UNIVERSALLY DESIGNED
LEADERSHIP
Applying UDL to Systems and Schools

BY **Katie Novak**
AND **Kristan Rodriguez**

UNIVERSALLY

DESIGNED

LEADERSHIP

Applying UDL to Systems and Schools

CAST Professional Publishing

UNTIL LEARNING HAS NO LIMITS™

Library of Congress Control Number: 2016944366
ISBN (Paperback) 978-1-930583-62-7
ISBN (Ebook) 978-1-930583-63-4

Published by:

CAST Professional Publishing
an imprint of CAST, Inc.
Wakefield, Massachusetts, USA

For information about special discounts for bulk purchases, please contact publishing@cast.org or telephone 781-245-2212 or visit *www.castpublishing.org*

Author photos: Felix and Sara Photographers

Cover and interior design by Happenstance Type-O-Rama.

Printed in the United States of America.

Contents

Introduction

We live in a world of great possibility. Our task as educational leaders is to collaborate with multiple stakeholders to design schools that build knowledge, grit, and creativity, all while challenging and engaging all learners, regardless of their differences. This is no easy task. An increased focus on rigorous college- and career-ready standards, educator evaluation, and standardized testing coupled with decreased resources makes this task akin to building a forest in a concrete jungle. Luckily, possibility and determination can conquer any obstacle: Shubhendu Sharma is proof.

Sharma (2014), an industrial engineer by trade, was inspired to design a platform to allow companies to build multilayer forests in concrete jungles. His company, Afforest, has done this—literally. Afforest can build lush, dense, forests of 300 or more trees in schools, factories, and even concrete areas equivalent to the size of six parking spaces. Sharma's forests improve air quality and increase biodiversity. And the cost? Similar to a smart phone. How is this possible? In a popular TED talk, Sharma explains: "To make afforestation as a mainstream business or an industry, we had to standardize the process of forest-making."

And he did just that. For Sharma, however, that was only the beginning: "Today, we are making forests in houses, in schools, even in factories with the corporates. But that's not enough. There are a huge number of people who want to take matters into their own hands." He goes on to explain that his company's next step is to create an Internet platform to guide others to build these forests, regardless of any obstacles they may encounter. His methodology will help anyone test their soil, identify their native species, and monitor their progress to ensure long-term success.

As educational leaders, we too aspire to build great systems in a landscape of barriers. To do this well, we also need a standardized process of building successful school districts. We need a process based on research and best-practice that allows us to "test our soil," "identify our native species," and monitor our long-term success so the process is personalized for our very unique landscape. Universal Design for Learning (UDL) allows us to do just that.

To begin this important work, we need to explore our landscape. CAST, the organization that defined and developed the UDL framework, identifies five phases of UDL implementation (National Center on Universal Design for Learning, 2012). These phases are Explore, Prepare, Integrate, Scale, and Optimize (Figure I.1).

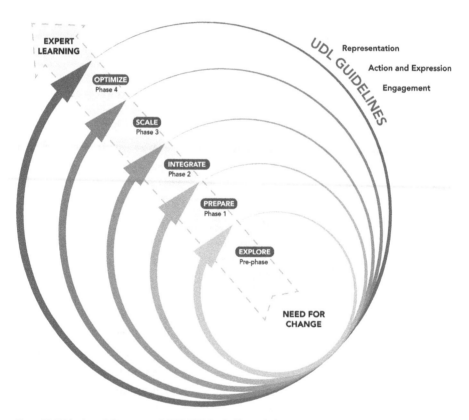

Figure I.1: UDL implementation process © CAST, 2012. Used with permission.

In Table I.1, we lay out the specific tasks associated with each phase of the process.

Table I.1: Phases and tasks of UDL implementation

Phase	Tasks
Explore	1. Investigate UDL as a potential system-wide decision-making framework. 2. Build awareness about UDL with key players within and outside of the system. 3. Determine willingness and interest of staff to begin district-wide UDL implementation.
Prepare	1. Create a climate that is flexible, but maintains high expectations for all. 2. Map needed resources and processes (i.e., specific personnel, and structures such as planning time, materials, curriculum, and professional development). 3. Define a strategic vision, plan of action, and expected outcomes.
Integrate	1. Create individual and system-wide structures and processes to support implementation, and evaluate its effectiveness. 2. Develop educator expertise, and apply UDL to instructional practices and decision-making. 3. Foster collaboration and support to integrate UDL broadly.
Scale	1. Promote ongoing professional growth by supporting a UDL community of practice that is responsive to individual and systemic variability. 2. Expand effective practices, processes, and structures through advanced professional development and technical assistance. 3. Enhance an integrated, system-wide approach to UDL implementation through continual evaluation of gaps and needs.
Optimize	1. Enhance a system-wide culture that aims to maximize improvement of teaching and learning practices in a way that reflects and aligns with the UDL principles. 2. Predict, prepare for, and respond to potential internal and external changes that could impact UDL implementation in the future. 3. Maximize improvement by embedding processes that respond to variability that exists within the system.

This book will focus on the first three implementation phases: Explore, Prepare, and Integrate. Our goal is to help education leaders learn why UDL is important, what groundwork needs to be laid to implement UDL, and how to start to build the system. A second volume, *Universally Designed Leadership: Next Steps*, will focus on the Scale and Optimize phases, which will support you as your forest begins to flourish.

1

Building Your Understanding

We introduce the Explore phase by providing a framework for how one can investigate UDL as a system-wide decision-making tool. This chapter will highlight critical features of UDL, present the "must-knows" for an administrative team, and showcase concrete examples of how UDL aligns with important district initiatives such as multi-tiered systems of support (MTSS), positive behavioral interventions and supports (PBIS), college- and career-ready standards, and educator evaluation. Creating this crosswalk will optimize relevance for districts and minimize the threat of adopting "another" initiative.

> *Gravity:* the force of attraction by which terrestrial bodies tend to fall toward the center of the earth.

The Next Generation Science Standards (NGSS Lead States, 2013) require students in grades six through eight to learn about gravity. Specifically, students are expected to "Develop and use a model to describe the role of gravity in the motions within galaxies and the solar system" (MS-ESS1-2). Oh, the gravity unit. Your own schooling probably included a teacher balanced on a metal chair who dropped objects of various mass as you plotted data on graph paper. At some point, you came to understand that heavier objects fall faster than objects with less mass. That elusive concept, gravity, became tangible, and you understood it. But not really. There was so much more to it than that.

Michael Brooks (2015), a bestselling author with a PhD in quantum physics, tells us that gravity remains our least-understood force in the universe. He aims to simplify the concept of gravity, to take what we know about it and communicate it to the masses so that collectively we will understand why, when we throw a ball into the air, it comes back down to earth.

The concept of leadership is similar to gravity. We all know that a leader is a person who leads a group, but becoming a highly effective, engaging, emotionally intelligent leader is a process that is not widely understood. Our work, like the work of Brooks, is to help to quantify the strategies that allow good leaders to become great.

Like gravity, great leaders are a force that can pull together their colleagues to create a highly functioning system. And now, it is more important than ever for leaders to have this ability. Schools must adapt to new models, such as MTSS, college- and career-ready standards, new methods of teacher evaluation, and an increased emphasis on getting results for all students despite increased student variability and decreased funding.

All these variables have the potential to decelerate a district's or school's progress, but this does not have to be the case. With effective leadership, all initiatives can be purposely connected to maximize the outcomes for all students and create a system that meets the needs of all stakeholders.

So, what does this system look like? Research tells us there are three core competencies of high-performing school systems (Curtis & City, 2009). These systems 1) understand where they are and where they are going, 2) develop a theory of action to support planning and strategy development, and 3) find ways to sustain improvement. These three competencies, however, are only effective if they are implemented with fidelity. A 500-page strategic plan with hundreds of initiatives will do nothing more than make heads spin. If we want to accelerate a district's progress and build a strong culture, we, as leaders, must commit to a few deep and meaningful goals. However, we can't develop these goals in isolation. Our teachers, our students, our families, and our communities are part of our system, and we owe it to them to develop meaningful goals that align to a shared vision. Therefore, as a first step, it's important to ask ourselves one question: *Does our vision truly reflect what our stakeholders want us to become?*

Reflect on that question and then dig deeper. Do your district's articulated mission and vision statements encompass the needs and hopes of all students, regardless of their variability? Are they grounded in scientific research and aligned to the values of all stakeholders? Or are they compliance heavy or born from a pool of shallow data about your district's strengths and needs?

Most of us lie somewhere in between, and that is not good enough. If we want to create a system where a force or vision pulls us all together, where all students are engaged in meaningful, challenging learning experiences that will allow them to excel in our world, we have to become resourceful, knowledgeable learners to explore what is possible, and then dare to achieve it. To do this, we need to foster collaboration and community with all stakeholders.

We learned this by accident. Upon reviewing the district's draft vision statement, a member of our community asked us if it was audacious enough. Having led the development of the vision, we defensively said, "YES, yes it is!" But the question nagged at us. So we unpacked our vision statement and a sinking feeling began to creep in.

Originally, we asked two questions: "What works?" and "What do we need to work on?" This led the community to answer in ways that were narrowed to our own experiences in our district. This was the data we reviewed when we crafted our vision statement. In the process, however, we failed to ask an important question: "What do we want to become?" Knowing where we stand is important. It is the first step, but it is not the destination. Had we not listened to that single inquiry, we may have moved ahead in developing a strategy that was not innovative. But, alas, we stopped. We listened, and we engaged our community.

We knew that if our future vision was to align with the principles of Universal Design for Learning, we would have to model UDL throughout the process. For us, the Explore phase began. As we set out to learn about the future of our district, we were committed to building awareness of UDL and its ability to lead us to wherever we decided to go.

***

When considering your vision for applying UDL, consider the future, while understanding the past and current conditions. One really helpful tool was a simple online survey that asked the community to review our vision statement. The survey was adapted from the "Vision Assessment Tool" (Curtis & City, 2009). The survey shared the current vision statement and asked members of the staff, students, and community to consider this vision in regard to how all-encompassing it is, how multi-dimensional it is, if it is shared, if it is clear, and if it is audacious. They were also offered a space to provide open-ended comments. Upon reviewing this feedback, we knew that our vision fell short. What would have happened if we had not listened to the feedback? We may have slipped into complacency about our already positive performance without embracing the needs of all learners.

To ensure that our vision and our plan for UDL is truly great, we must create a framework for information-based decision-making. We must also keep instructional improvement front and center. If we do so, UDL will be a guidepost in the development of the three competencies of effective systems: understanding the work (the "what"), knowing how to do the work (the "how"), and creating a culture for continual improvement, sustained engagement, and self-reflection (the "why"). Though UDL is still a new concept to many districts, the framework itself is based on decades of peer-reviewed research in the neurosciences and learning sciences (Meyer, Rose, & Gordon, 2014). In addition, UDL implementation in schools and districts has shown very promising returns in recent years (see, for example, the November 2015 issue of *School Administrator* magazine and van Horn, 2015).

Regardless of your background in UDL, it will soon become an important part of your district strategy. The Every Student Succeeds Act (ESSA) urges states to adopt UDL in a number of areas. For example, it says assessments should be designed using the principles of UDL. It also requires schools to "use technology, consistent with the principles of universal design for learning, to support the learning needs of all students, including children with disabilities and English learners" (ESSA, 2015, Section 4104). UDL will be playing a larger role in our everyday practice moving forward. This book will provide you with a road map for how to incorporate it into your work as a means to ensure student success.

The formula that allows scientists to understand how gravity works is called the universal gravitational constant (Kantha, 2012). Just as the universal gravitational constant gives us a formula to make sense of gravity, UDL provides administrators with a formula to become effective leaders. Universally designed leadership is built upon three guiding principles, divided into the nine UDL Guidelines (CAST, 2011). Understanding these principles and Guidelines is the first concrete step in pulling a system together to create a strategy to meet the needs of all students.

Guiding Principles

As school- or district-level administrators, we are tasked with leading large groups of stakeholders with significant variability among and within respective groups. Our challenge is to ensure that we present information to all parties in ways that are accessible to them, allow multiple channels for two-way communication, and engage everyone in the process.

Neuroscience research tells us that in order for someone to learn, there are three networks of the brain that must be activated: the recognition network, the strategic network, and the affective network (Meyer, Rose, & Gordon, 2014; Rose & Meyer, 2002). These networks allow learners to interpret new information; plan, execute, and express that information; and remain engaged throughout the learning process. If we, as administrators, cannot activate these networks in our stakeholders, we will not have a community of expert learners. Think of it as a constant, like gravity.

The three UDL principles correspond to the learning networks: provide multiple means of representation (the "what"), provide multiple means of action and expression (the "how"), and provide multiple means of engagement (the "why"; Rose & Meyer, 2002). Right away, you will notice an alignment to the three central competencies of a successful system (Figure 1.1). Applying the three principles of UDL, therefore, is imperative as districts develop a strategy to improve the outcomes of all students.

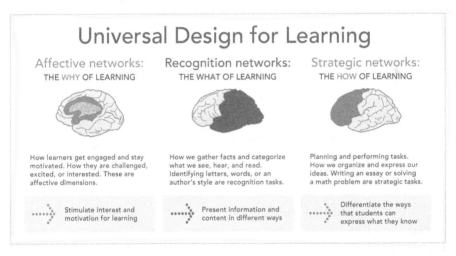

Universal Design for Learning

Affective networks:
THE WHY OF LEARNING

Recognition networks:
THE WHAT OF LEARNING

Strategic networks:
THE HOW OF LEARNING

How learners get engaged and stay motivated. How they are challenged, excited, or interested. These are affective dimensions.

How we gather facts and categorize what we see, hear, and read. Identifying letters, words, or an author's style are recognition tasks.

Planning and performing tasks. How we organize and express our ideas. Writing an essay or solving a math problem are strategic tasks.

Stimulate interest and motivation for learning

Present information and content in different ways

Differentiate the ways that students can express what they know

Figure 1.1: Three learning networks © 2013. CAST, Inc. All rights reserved.

Imagine the value of all teachers, parents, community members, and students understanding important district initiatives for curriculum and instruction, the district's vision or strategy, the district's budget, and day-to-day announcements such as the release date for report cards, the cafeteria menu, and where to submit health forms. In order for this to happen, we need to activate the recognition network of our community by providing multiple means of representation—which includes presenting information in multiple and accessible formats but also extends to activating background knowledge, providing support for cultural differences in understanding, and so forth.

For example, many districts post a newly adopted vision statement on their website, send an announcement via e-mail, post to social media outlets, or have an automated system to send a voice or text message to phones. Although this is a step in the right direction, this mass dissemination only ensures that parties perceive information. Perception alone does not result in learning. It's similar to the concept of gravity—if we throw a ball in the air, we know it will come down, but it may not land exactly where we expect.

Providing multiple means of representation, therefore, requires us to present information in ways that allow all stakeholders to recognize predictive patterns in that information, understand and integrate new information within their current understanding, interpret and manipulate that information, and develop fluency in the skills for assimilating and remembering that information (Meyer, Rose, & Gordon, 2014). There is a lot more work to do, therefore, to get all stakeholders to learn about important district work and become an integral part of our system.

The second principle reminds us to provide multiple means for action and expression to activate the strategic network. This is not just a reminder to provide options for stakeholders to communicate with us. Opening lines of communication is a step in the right direction, but in order to get valuable, relevant feedback from all stakeholders, and to ensure that they are becoming experts in understanding our district, our vision, and our work, we need to support the development of executive functions, their own strategy development, and the management of resources. Imagine, for example, that you want to collect feedback on your district vision. Assuming you communicate the vision using multiple means of representation, you will need a system in place for all stakeholders to express their feedback back to you. If you've attempted a project like this before, you know how this anecdote ends. Even if you send an e-mail and host an open forum, you have many teachers, staff members, parents, students, and community members who will not respond. The reasons why are too numerous to list, but they can be categorized under two UDL principles. One, they did not have an appropriate strategy to respond (i.e., they did not set a goal, did not manage their time to complete the goal), or they were not engaged in the task and therefore, they did not feel it was relevant or authentic.

That leads us to the third UDL principle: provide multiple means of engagement to activate the affective network. When stakeholders are engaged with us, they are interested in what we have to share, have a purpose for learning, are motivated to learn and participate, and have self-regulation strategies so they can be reflective throughout the process. What makes this task difficult is the significant variability among and within stakeholder groups. Therefore, as we provide multiple means of representation and expression, we must adjust demands and the levels of challenge and provide different levels of support, so everyone has the skills necessary to persist in the learning experience and become an integral part of our system.

When the district sets a path for future work, a vision for future success, and an articulated mission and set of core values, it is defining, in a concrete manner, its priorities in education. A goal of this work is to build awareness with stakeholders about the need for UDL. It is helpful to pair this future work with an articulated process of defining existing needs. In regards to the needs definition, we recommend a comprehensive needs assessment. This needs assessment will articulate for the community the areas of need. For example: Is there a gap in the performance of special education and general education students? What are the district's overall performance needs? Are the social and emotional needs of the students being met? How does the district compare with high-performing districts? The answers to these questions will define a platform of need, which UDL can help to address. It is important to remember that both the needs assessment and the exploration of a defined vision for the future should be universally designed. We, as leaders, must keep the success of all as our focus as we include the voices of the greater community and strive toward continuous improvement.

When building a shared vision for the future work of the district, we should design an inclusive plan, implement the plan, monitor progress, and refine the strategy. Although all UDL principles will be present in all aspects of the plan, you can see how the four steps align closely with particular UDL principles.

Table 1.1: Shared vision and UDL alignment

Activity	UDL Alignment
Design a plan for shared vision work.	Provide multiple means of engagement by optimizing relevance, value, and authenticity as you consider all stakeholders and their involvement. Provide multiple means of action and expression by guiding appropriate goal-setting and planning for strategy development.
Implement shared vision process.	Provide multiple means of action and expression by guiding appropriate goal-setting and providing options for various levels of support so all stakeholders can be involved in meaningful ways.

Table 1.1: Shared vision and UDL alignment (continued)

Activity	UDL Alignment
Monitor progress during the process.	Provide multiple means of engagement by developing self-assessment and reflection, and encouraging mastery-oriented feedback.
Adapt process as necessary.	Provide multiple means of action and expression so all stakeholders have opportunities to contribute.

UDL Guidelines

Each of the three UDL principles has three corresponding Guidelines. These nine Guidelines provide more specific ways for us to provide multiple means of representation, expression, and engagement to our stakeholders. Table 1.2 identifies the Guidelines and highlights the big ideas of each guideline and its implications for administrators.

Table 1.2: UDL Guidelines and their implications

To Activate the Brain: Adhere to UDL Principles →	To Adhere to UDL Principles: Implement Guidelines →	Clarification and Big Ideas for Guidelines
Provide multiple means of representation.	Provide options for perception.	Information is more easily accessed when it is in multiple formats. For example, when sharing a curriculum adoption summary with teachers, it would be valuable to have a written report, a one-page synopsis or Powerpoint, and a video or short audio explanation.

Table 1.2: UDL Guidelines and their implications (continued)

To Activate the Brain: Adhere to UDL Principles →	To Adhere to UDL Principles: Implement Guidelines →	Clarification and Big Ideas for Guidelines
	Provide options for language, mathematical expressions, and symbols.	Because stakeholders vary widely in their understanding of symbols, acronyms, and vocabulary, it's important to clarify important terms, define acronyms, and use short narratives to explain symbols, charts, and graphs. Your school board, for example, may not know the meaning of the veritable alphabet soup that educating our children has become—MTSS, UDL, PBIS—so make these definitions clear.
	Provide options for comprehension.	Constructing knowledge is an active process, so when we present new information to district stakeholders, we must strategically categorize this information so they know where new information integrates with their prior knowledge. For example, if you refine your district vision, it may be helpful to share a "crosswalk," where you note which aspects of the original vision were revised with an explanation for the changes.
Provide multiple means of action and expression.	Provide options for physical action.	Provide opportunities for your stakeholders to get up and collaborate in person, interact with online modules, or use assistive technology to communicate with you. Physical action is an important component of active learning, so provide options when presenting to teachers and staff, parents, and community members.

Table 1.2: UDL Guidelines and their implications (continued)

To Activate the Brain: Adhere to UDL Principles →	To Adhere to UDL Principles: Implement Guidelines →	Clarification and Big Ideas for Guidelines
	Provide options for expression and communication.	Open multiple channels and venues for stakeholders to communicate and interact with you. Be prepared to read e-mails, tweets, Facebook posts, and handwritten letters. Make and answer phone calls, and have meetings in common areas where people can come to talk in person. Present in school libraries, in senior centers, and be available for a chat in a local diner.
	Provide options for executive functions.	We need to help stakeholders set concrete goals for their contributions. We can do this by providing exemplars for the type of information or product we're looking for, checklists and prompts to help guide them, and clarity in our call to action. Do you want community members to share their vision for the schools? Make it clear. Write a sample response, give parameters for how to write a vision, or give examples they can agree or disagree with.
Provide multiple means of engagement.	Provide options for recruiting interest.	You need to attract people's attention before you can teach them anything or share information with them. To craft a message that recruits stakeholders of vast variability, provide a variety of messages and calls to action that are age-appropriate, culturally relevant, and contextualized.

Table 1.2: UDL Guidelines and their implications (continued)

To Activate the Brain: Adhere to UDL Principles →	To Adhere to UDL Principles: Implement Guidelines →	Clarification and Big Ideas for Guidelines
	Provide options for sustaining effort and persistence.	Recruiting interest is one thing. Maintaining interest is the greater challenge. In order to keep all parties engaged in our system, we have to consistently share our goals and objectives, foster collaboration and community, and provide feedback on our process.
	Provide options for self-regulation.	Lastly, we must develop self-assessment and reflection in ourselves so we can model that to our district community. An effective system is a well-oiled machine, with strategies in place for coping when new initiatives or new research surfaces. Every strategic plan must be frequently assessed and adapted, as necessary, based on rich information sources, so the district can cope with the ever-changing world of education.

Each of the nine UDL Guidelines has affiliated checkpoints—specific actions to support UDL implementation (Figure 1.2).

Universal Design for Learning Guidelines

Provide Multiple Means of

Engagement

Purposeful, motivated learners

Provide options for self-regulation
+ Promote expectations and beliefs that optimize motivation
+ Facilitate personal coping skills and strategies
+ Develop self-assessment and reflection

Provide options for sustaining effort and persistence
+ Heighten salience of goals and objectives
+ Vary demands and resources to optimize challenge
+ Foster collaboration and community
+ Increase mastery-oriented feedback

Provide options for recruiting interest
+ Optimize individual choice and autonomy
+ Optimize relevance, value, and authenticity
+ Minimize threats and distractions

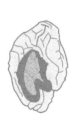

Provide Multiple Means of

Representation

Resourceful, knowledgeable learners

Provide options for comprehension
+ Activate or supply background knowledge
+ Highlight patterns, critical features, big ideas, and relationships
+ Guide information processing, visualization, and manipulation
+ Maximize transfer and generalization

Provide options for language, mathematical expressions, and symbols
+ Clarify vocabulary and symbols
+ Clarify syntax and structure
+ Support decoding of text, mathematical notation, and symbols
+ Promote understanding across languages
+ Illustrate through multiple media

Provide options for perception
+ Offer ways of customizing the display of information
+ Offer alternatives for auditory information
+ Offer alternatives for visual information

Provide Multiple Means of

Action & Expression

Strategic, goal-directed learners

Provide options for executive functions
+ Guide appropriate goal-setting
+ Support planning and strategy development
+ Enhance capacity for monitoring progress

Provide options for expression and communication
+ Use multiple media for communication
+ Use multiple tools for construction and composition
+ Build fluencies with graduated levels of support for practice and performance

Provide options for physical action
+ Vary the methods for response and navigation
+ Optimize access to tools and assistive technologies

Figure 1.2: UDL Guidelines, 2.0. © 2013 CAST. Used with permission.

UDL as a System-Wide Decision-Making Tool

To build a district, leaders need the input and commitment of all stakeholders. Our teachers, colleagues, and district community are often adept at identifying our general investment as leaders as new initiatives come our way. If they feel a new initiative is a passing fad or a mandate from above, they will tread water until a new wave rolls in. If we, as leaders, can't provide options to recruit and sustain their interest, they will not become purposeful and motivated to invest in an initiative, and the initiative will fail. So, how can we increase engagement as we explore UDL as a district framework? We have to become expert learners ourselves and model the UDL Guidelines in all aspects of our practice.

For example, when teachers participate in professional development, are you in attendance, demonstrating your commitment to learning? If you are not, consider what your absence communicates to your colleagues. In order to provide the support for UDL, you must understand the framework and how its implementation will affect all aspects of your district strategy. One such way to demonstrate investment is to know what you are talking about. Understand the UDL Guidelines and the research that supports them. Be able to speak to the benefits of UDL for all learners, and share and present this information to staff in a universally designed manner.

Now begins the first phase of UDL implementation: Explore. If you're reading this book, you are beginning the Explore phase, but it's important that your district is able to explore collectively. During this phase, you will need to be purposeful in providing a framework for how your district can utilize UDL as a system-wide decision-making tool. The biggest mistake is introducing UDL in isolation. This can lead to the perception that UDL is "just another initiative." To avoid this, it's important to develop a strategy for this phase. In our own district, we began the Explore phase by introducing the UDL framework to our leadership team in a two-day summer workshop. The organization of the retreat was universally designed and aligned to all UDL Guidelines. Throughout the retreat, we made explicit connections to how the UDL framework would support us as we developed a district strategy to meet the needs of all learners. Although the agenda was universally designed, a two-day retreat is not enough to sustain engagement throughout the Explore phase. Thus, at the retreat, we included resources to communicate how the retreat topics would be interwoven into bimonthly leadership team meetings, and highlighted how UDL aligns with all other district initiatives. This scaffolding is essential to minimize the threat of adopting another initiative that will pass without increasing student outcomes or district effectiveness.

The Explore phase is just the beginning, but you have to start somewhere. Pulling a system together to maximize student learning is not easy, but it is important work. To improve our schools, we must understand the work ahead of us, know how to do the work, and build a system of improvement and continued engagement. To drive toward audaciousness in our vision, our strategy, and our outcomes for all students, we have to ask ourselves three questions: "What?" "How?" and "Why?" The answer to all three is the same: universally designed leadership.

Tying It All Together

To combat initiative fatigue, we must ensure that all the work we do by choice supports the mandated work we are required to accomplish. Below is a crosswalk that aligns sample statewide initiatives to UDL. We encourage you to develop a similar crosswalk with the work in which your district is engaged. The intent behind such a crosswalk is to demonstrate that UDL is a means to accomplish all other initiatives.

Table 1.3: Example of an initiative-UDL crosswalk

Initiative	UDL Alignment
Multi-Tiered System of Supports (MTSS)	The Massachusetts Department of Elementary and Secondary Education (DESE) requires all districts to offer a single system of support that is responsive to the needs of all students, regardless of variability. This approach is built on a model where all students are offered universally designed curriculum, instruction, and assessments in Tier I that include options for differentiated support and extension activities. All learning experiences in Tier I are designed for all students and offer multiple means of representation, multiple means of action and expression, and multiple means of engagement. When Tier I is implemented with fidelity, it minimizes the number of students who need Tier II support, the goal of which is to remediate academic skill deficits with the idea that in doing so, students will be successful in the Tier I program without support (Johnson, 2015).
	When curriculum, instruction, and assessments in Tier II are universally designed, fewer students will require Tier III intervention, which is more explicit, focuses on remediation of skills, is provided for a longer duration of time (both in overall length of intervention and regularly scheduled minutes of instructional time), and occurs in smaller groups (i.e., groups of 1-3 students; Harlacher & Sanford, 2015).
	All three tiers in the MTSS model are flexible in nature, as students have opportunities to access instruction in all three tiers simultaneously.

Table 1.3: Example of an initiative-UDL crosswalk (continued)

Initiative	UDL Alignment
Positive Behavioral Interventions and Supports (PBIS)	Like MTSS, PBIS is a multi-tiered system to service delivery, with all students receiving core services in Tier I that are universally designed to reach all students (Averill & Rinaldi, 2011). Like MTSS, Tier I includes teaching a set of appropriate behaviors to all students using multiple means of representation, action and expression, and engagement.
	When evidence suggests that Tier I instruction, even when universally designed, does not meet the needs of students, those students will receive Tier II support, in addition to Tier I services, which focuses on behavioral interventions. Students who require more intensive intervention for a longer duration will receive Tier III support, while also accessing Tier I and Tier II services.
New Curriculum Standards	Our state frameworks incorporate the Common Core State Standards. The Common Core (National Governors Association Center for Best Practices & Council of Chief State School Officers, 2010), in the section "Application to Students with Disabilities" notes, "Students eligible under the Individuals with Disabilities Education Act (IDEA)" must be challenged to excel within the general curriculum and be prepared for success in their post-school lives, including college and/or careers . . . . Therefore, how high standards are taught and assessed is of the utmost importance in reaching this diverse group of students."
	The key word is how. How will teachers design curriculum and instruction so that all students have equal opportunity to learn the same rigorous material? The same section offers a simple answer: Universal Design for Learning (UDL). UDL is defined as "a scientifically valid framework for guiding educational practice that (a) provides flexibility in the ways information is presented, in the ways students respond or demonstrate knowledge and skills, and in the ways students are engaged; and (b) reduces barriers in instruction, provides appropriate accommodations, supports, and challenges, and maintains high achievement expectations for all students, including students with disabilities and students who are limited English proficient," by the Higher Education Opportunity Act (PL 110-135).

Table 1.3: Example of an initiative-UDL crosswalk (continued)

Initiative	UDL Alignment
Educator Evaluation	If the district is going to integrate UDL districtwide, the educator evaluation system must integrate it smoothly. Evaluators must know what to look for, and staff must be trained in what to do. Below are some examples of how UDL can be integrated into educator evaluation. In our evaluation system, educators are expected to develop SMART goals, obtain observation feedback, and provide artifacts of practice. Here are ways we integrated UDL into these aspects of our evaluation model: <ul><li>We universally designed all of our educator evaluation training.</li><li>We provided training on UDL to all educators (teachers and administrators).</li><li>We provided exemplar educator goals written in the framework of UDL.</li><li>We provided samples of observation feedback, and forms that support the principles of UDL.</li><li>We provided exemplars of artifacts that are universally designed.</li><li>We focused on key aspects of the educator rubric that align directly with UDL.</li></ul>

Sharing how UDL is a vehicle to accomplish other important initiatives is a crucial step in the Explore phase. All stakeholders should understand that UDL is not another initiative, a "flavor of the month." Rather, UDL is an organizing mechanism that can bring the district's important work together so it all aligns to a shared vision for system-wide improvement—one that will ensure success for all students.

2

Using Evidence-Based Decision-Making to Begin the Work

This chapter will focus on an important aspect of the Explore phase: investigating UDL as a system-wide decision-making framework, and building awareness with key players inside and outside the system. The chapter will highlight the need for administrators to use a variety of quantitative and qualitative information to identify strengths and needs in the district before preparing for implementation. We will also highlight the importance of completing meaningful research on best-in-class districts to guide appropriate goal-setting.

In his famous lecture, "Society and Solitude," Ralph Waldo Emerson (1870) declared: "A man builds a fine house; and now he has a master, and a task for life; he is to furnish, watch, show it, and keep it in repair, the rest of his days." Emerson isn't just talking about building a house—his reference is to a *fine house*. But what distinguishes a house from a fine house? It's the foundation. An article from *This Old House* magazine (Alexander, 2015) reminds readers that foundations should last forever, so you have to make them right. Building a strong foundation for a house requires some customization: "[A] good foundation requires a lot more than digging a hole and pouring some concrete into forms. It must be tailored to its site like a custom suit, taking into account soil conditions, water tables, even the quality of the backfill. And as with a custom suit, every detail must be perfect: the base properly compacted, the formwork set up right, the concrete free of voids. Neglect even one of these, and the most carefully poured foundation can fail."

UDL needs to become the foundation upon which all district improvement initiatives are built. And just like a house's foundation is customized for the ground it sits on, UDL must be tailored for the district. This site work in your district will happen in the Explore phase. As you begin to explore UDL, you will investigate UDL as a system-wide decision-making framework and build awareness with key players inside and outside the system. To set this up right, administrators will need to use a variety of quantitative and qualitative information to identify strengths and needs in the district before preparing for implementation. The district will also need to complete meaningful research on best-in-class districts to guide appropriate goal-setting.

Collaborating with district stakeholders to build a needs assessment is a crucial step during the Explore phase. Specifically, we suggest the following action steps:

1. Use thematic coding of attitudinal data from stakeholders to build consensus and engagement.

2. Report data out in meaningful and accessible ways using multiple means of representation.

3. Demonstrate a bridge among information-gathering, district and school goals, and action plan development.

Before you can begin this work, however, there is some site work to be done. As with our fine house, we must remember: "Neglect even one of these, and the most carefully poured foundation can fail" (Alexander, 2015).

In this chapter, we will break down the process of engaging in site work for a needs assessment, which will prepare the site for the UDL foundation. If you lay a faulty foundation, the structure will crumble. Laying the right foundation is time-consuming and it takes strong leadership to allow the time, energy, and resources to be spent.

Table 2.1: Checklist for preparing for data analysis: Needs assessment site work protocol for UDL work

Place ✔ Here	Data Analysis Preparation Steps	Alignment to UDL
	Understand your data culture	• Highlight patterns, critical features, big ideas, and relationships • Optimize relevance, value, and authenticity • Develop self-assessment and reflection
	Create norms for evidence-based conversations	• Maximize transfer and generalization • Minimize threats and distractions • Foster collaboration and community • Increase mastery-oriented feedback

Table 2.1: Checklist for preparing for data analysis: Needs assessment site work protocol for UDL work (continued)

Place ✔ Here	Data Analysis Preparation Steps	Alignment to UDL
	Determine protocols prior to data collection	• Guide appropriate goal-setting • Support planning and strategy development • Facilitate managing information and resources • Enhance capacity for monitoring progress
	Define best-in-class districts	• Heighten salience of goals and objectives
	Determine and articulate weaknesses in data collection methods	• Provide options for language, mathematical expressions, and symbols • Minimize threats and distractions
	Identifying themes in data collection	• Highlight patterns, critical features, big ideas, and relationships
	Design framework to communicate the work	• Maximize transfer and generalization • Guide appropriate goal-setting • Support planning and strategy development

Understand Your Data Culture

In recent years, we have seen the term *data-based decision-making* go from an unknown concept to one that can sometimes have negative connotations of unfair accountability measures and judgments. In our experience, this has less to do with the data itself and more to do with the context and application of the data. Fear of data suggests a faulty foundation, where data-based decision-making was not introduced in the context of value, or was used too narrowly. UDL must be used to build a foundation of evidence-based decision-making; we believe the term *data-based decision-making* is too narrow. The concept of evidence-based decision-making wraps attitudinal data, quantitative data, and research together. It embeds the concepts of the logic model (Curtis & City, 2009) and has an outcome of defined SMART goals and an actionable and accountable plan. It begins with norm development that sets the stage for inquiry in a safe and effective manner.

In your district, you will need all stakeholders to be involved in improvement planning and UDL implementation. Understanding the variability of your own district is imperative so you can provide options to meet the needs of stakeholders regardless of their level of commitment, expertise, and background knowledge. Before beginning the Explore phase, it's important to understand why evidence-based decision-making is crucial.

Building a framework for understanding the purpose for data use, or the use of evidence, is an essential precursor to this needs assessment. As a first step, it is valuable to understand the dynamic of the leadership and learning matrix. Reeves (2008) developed the leadership and learning matrix to distinguish our efforts as leaders in four categories (Figure 2.1).

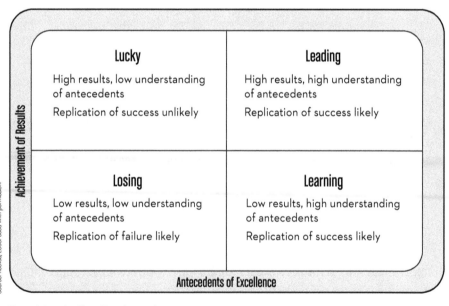

Figure 2.1: Leadership and learning matrix

The matrix articulates results data against the antecedents and categorizes our efforts into being lucky, losing, learning, or leading. We, as leaders, strive to be in the leading quadrant, as this assumes a high ability to replicate our results. If we frame our work around data and evidence so the efforts are demonstrated to inform our practice and increase outcomes for students, the work becomes meaningful to all stakeholders. A systemic process for data use must be established. Defined in that process are the ways we explore data, the structures to allow data analysis to occur, and defined products. Do we, as leaders, have a basis for effective data meetings? Have we invested time and energy to provide professional development (PD) in data use? Do we have systems in place to allow all staff, regardless of variability, to engage in instructional data meetings? Do we have centralized data clearinghouses? These very technical pieces should be established prior to implementing an evidence-based approach to our work. Beyond these technical pieces, though, is the heart of the push-back around information use in our schools. Uncovering information about our performance is a very personal pursuit that often occurs in public forums with colleagues.

In order to build a culture of shared evidence-based decision-making, it's important to first gather important information about your district's data culture and what your community needs in order to embrace evidence. Your task, during this process, is to gather information to start conversations about data, and use these conversations as a springboard as you build a sustainable plan for UDL.

In our district, we began this work with our teachers. After a short presentation on our district improvement plan, we asked teachers to respond to prompts about our current data culture (Table 2.2).

Table 2.2: Evidence-based decision-making site work prompts

UDL Site Work Prompts
• What are your current feelings about how this district uses data to impact instruction? Please be candid in your response.
• What specific steps would we need to take to make data conversations more meaningful in your school or department?
• What barriers do we face if we want all stakeholders to have important conversations about data and how that data impacts instruction?
• Please describe the culture of your school or department.
• What would need to change in your culture in order for all parties to embrace evidence-based decision-making?
• What ongoing professional development would we need to support a culture of evidence-based decision-making in our district?
• What would all leaders need to understand in order to support evidence-based decision-making in our district?

In our own work, these questions yielded valuable evidence about our district's data culture. For example, one important theme that we highlighted was that our staff felt as though too many initiatives came and went with each new administration. Many staff members noted the district's habit of moving from one initiative to the next without ever sticking with one. Many felt that data-based decision-making was just another initiative. This was imperative for us to know as we began planning so we could address this head on. We knew that one obstacle we would face was the perception that data-based decision-making was another passing fad, so we were sure to highlight this barrier to ensure that our process was valuable to our staff.

Exploring the district culture and perception of data is imperative in order to minimize the threat of data. It provides leaders with an understanding of where the district is starting, and will allow for the meaningful development of opportunities to continue to explore data in an authentic way.

It is no surprise that people avoid data-based discussions because it often feels like an analysis and attack of their own work. We do not know any educators (effective or not) who go to work thinking they are doing a bad job. By dissecting information that demonstrates areas of strength and challenge, we are uncovering something intrinsically personal, and exposing areas of need that undermine that educator's life's work. One UDL checkpoint reminds us to provide mastery-oriented feedback to support our stakeholders as they become purposeful, motivated learners. This feedback, however, can be tough to receive, especially if it activates one of the three triggers: truth, relationship, and identity (Stone & Heen, 2014). These triggers create barriers for accepting feedback and sustaining effort and persistence while exploring all data and evidence (see "Three Feedback Triggers" for more information). We need to understand the three triggers before we begin to analyze the data on teacher perceptions, so we can further minimize threats and distractions as we begin this work.

THREE FEEDBACK TRIGGERS

(Adapted from Stone & Heen, 2014)

The first trigger, *truth*, is when the feedback we are giving seems wrong, or based on incomplete data. For example, we may share college attendance rates with our school counselors, noting that there was a significant decline for two consecutive years without delving into cohort data. By providing incomplete data, there is a possibility that the information is simply a result of the cohort. When we provide feedback about how we would like to form a committee to begin the logic model process, we risk activating the truth trigger and losing engagement in an important process.

The second trigger, *relationships*, is when the receiver does not believe we are a reliable source, or that we do not truly understand the situation. For example, imagine we provide the data on the decline in college attendance, and we include an analysis of cohort data. We then provide what we believe is mastery-oriented feedback. The numbers aren't enough if our counselors know, for example, that a number of students have been joining the military because of local recruiting efforts, and we did not. In this case, they may believe our data is accurate, but they don't believe we know enough about it to make meaningful conclusions.

The third trigger, *identity*, is when the feedback is just too overwhelming and threatens the identity of the receiver. They believe that what we say is true, and that we understand the situation, but they aren't ready to hear that feedback. In the example above, imagine we provide the cohort data and highlight the patterns of students who choose to join the military, and have enough information to show that these variables did not contribute to the decline. After this analysis, we provide our mastery-oriented feedback, but when we do, our counselors may become defensive because of the identity trigger.

Create Norms for Evidence-Based Conversations

If we aspire to have meaningful conversations and make evidence-based decisions, we must first eliminate the barriers and triggers that have the potential to threaten our process. This is again where our work must be built on the UDL framework. We cannot build engagement in the evidence-based decision-making approach if we do not provide options for self-regulation. Specifically, we need to provide expectations and beliefs that optimize motivation, facilitate coping skills and strategies, and develop reflection throughout the process. This work can be done by creating thoughtful norms to frame this process.

To provide expectations that optimize motivation and minimize threats, we suggest schools and district be purposeful and careful to distinguish meeting expectations from thoughtful norms. Many people define items such as "arriving on time and having an agenda" as a norm. Although this is important so that people do not feel that their time is wasted, this fits into the category of meeting expectations. In our work, items such as these do little to change the framework of the discourse and get the team into a place to have deep and meaningful conversations. Establishing meeting expectations is easier and can be done first. Establishing meaningful norms about how we discuss this sensitive work is an essential next step if we are to create a culture where our colleagues are motivated to participate in this process.

There are a number of tools that can help you develop norms to minimize the three feedback triggers mentioned previously. If you are not up to the task of developing individualized norms, authors like Love, Stiles, Mundry, and DiRanna (2008) have defined and provided packaged norms and accompanying resources to introduce and execute these norms. There are also free resources such as those on the National School Reform Faculty (2015) site that provide protocols to norm-setting.

Upon the backs of these norms, the group can roll up their sleeves and get to work to review evidence and begin to share mastery-oriented feedback with one another without activating one of the three feedback triggers. Many districts went from a place of not having any data to swimming in too much of it. Our experience has demonstrated that most districts have a lot of some forms of data, very little data in other areas, sparse tools to analyze qualitative data, and an almost nonexistent use of research data. For example, a district may have a lot of elementary-level literacy data, may have developed math benchmarks, and may have easily accessible state and national secondary data in ELA, math, and science. Yet, they do not have meaningful data in the areas of elementary social studies, fine and performing arts, and social and emotional learning. They may lack growth data in science, or may have never done a vetted and thoughtful review of research into world language instruction. For example, how many districts have subscriptions to scholarly research and university-level research sites, and regularly have administrators use the review of peer-reviewed or scholarly articles as a regular component of their decision-making? Without all of this information, our evidence is incomplete, and as we mentioned previously, it is likely that we will activate the truth trigger and we will not be able to move forward.

The need to explore quantitative data, qualitative data, and research is an essential triangulation in the needs-assessment phase. The readiness of the team is an important understanding in engaging in this work. If a team member or the team as a whole do not have the background to effectively do this work independently, then the group must engage in this work collectively and build fluencies, with graduated levels of support for practice and performance. What do we mean by this? Key stakeholders in this work include the administrative team. They need to model and lead this work at their schools and in their departments. Using a framework of collective inquiry, they must engage in district improvement planning that embeds this work and models it. This will maximize transfer and generalization, which will allow the administrative team to become resourceful, knowledgeable leaders who can provide exemplars for other staff members.

Determine Protocols Prior to Data Collection

The UDL Guidelines remind us to guide appropriate goal-setting to support planning and strategy development. Once you explore your district's data culture and begin to build norms with all stakeholders, it's time to begin to develop a strategy for the upcoming data work. During this stage, it's important for teams to identify the types of data they will review, identify the processes for stakeholder participation and vetting, and determine how results will be shared throughout the process.

First, it's valuable for teams to determine which data, or evidence, they will review. Research has suggested that there are five sources of knowledge that can be used as evidence (Pawson et al., 2003). These sources were originally identified for the health-care field, but can be applied to the field of education, as well. The five sources are identified below and we have further defined them through an educational lens. We also identify specific types of data you may choose to collect in each category. Table 2.3 is certainly not an exhaustive list, but it will help refine the UDL focus areas. It should be articulated that this work will take months to complete and require a large stakeholder investment. When identifying which types of evidence to review, we suggest including a balance of evidence from each of the sources in order to connect research and practice.

Once you have identified the sources of evidence to collect, you must determine how you will involve all stakeholders in the collection and review of this evidence. It is not only important to collect knowledge from multiple stakeholders, but it's crucial to ask for their input in reviewing the data and any conclusions the team has made based on the evidence. The timeline for asking for stakeholder feedback will likely vary based on the data analysis procedures you undertake. Regardless, it is important to set a timeline where the team will ask for the input of all stakeholders at regular intervals to increase relevance and authenticity and provide multiple opportunities to monitor progress throughout the process.

Table 2.3: Sources of knowledge in educational data work

Source of Knowledge	Clarified through Educational Lens	Sample Data Sources
Organizational knowledge	Administrators need to have knowledge of many operational aspects of the organization, which may affect student outcomes. Gathering their knowledge is an important aspect to evidence collection.	• Individual and small group meetings with administration • A review of district and school improvement plans and goals • A review of the state report cards and/or accountability levels for the district and schools • A review of 10 years of budget reports and documents • A review of existing curriculum documents (e.g., scope/sequence, vision documents, maps) • A review of aggregated and disaggregated assessment results (at least five years of scores for each) • State audit reports for Title I, ELE, civil rights, and special education • A review of district and school websites • A review of the interview questions (to understand district's priorities) • A review of the job descriptions or essential job functions
Practitioner knowledge	Highly qualified educators provide an invaluable source of knowledge about the strengths, needs, and future vision of a school district. They can offer qualitative, observational data, as well as quantitative data, on student achievement and outcomes.	• Open forum and survey data on what is working and what needs work with staff • Staff surveys on working conditions • Staff surveys on existing professional development offerings • A review of staff evaluations

Table 2.3: Sources of knowledge in educational data work (continued)

Source of Knowledge	Clarified through Educational Lens	Sample Data Sources
User knowledge	Our students and families are also an important source of evidence. As the end users in education, students can share their perceptions about the quality of their education. Families also serve as important partners in this work.	• Open forum and survey data on what is working and what needs work with students and their families • Student achievement data including attendance and graduation rates, college acceptance rates, and so on
Research, gathered systematically with a planned design	Research argues that in the hierarchy of knowledge, research knowledge reigns supreme. When research is large-scale, peer-reviewed, and systematic, it is more reliable than other sources (Pawson et al., 2003). As leaders, we have access to research-based best practices through peer-reviewed journals, policy briefs, and national studies focused on improving the outcomes of identified populations of students.	• Peer-reviewed journal articles on best practices in curriculum and instruction • Specific data points from best-in-class districts including achievement data, financial data, and staffing data • Statistics from the National Center for Education Statistics • Review of findings from the International Benchmarking Association on international best practices
Knowledge gained from the wider policy context	Other important sources of knowledge are the artifacts that are developed at the district, state, or national level based on best practices. For example, the roll-out of evidence-based college- and career-ready standards, educator evaluation systems, and evidence-based curriculum and instructional tools are valuable to analyze with the other sources of data.	• Open forum and survey data on what is working with elected officials • School district policy handbook • State curriculum frameworks • State educator evaluation system • State and national educational laws

Define Best-in-Class Districts

Once you understand your data culture, set meaningful norms, and begin to determine the data collection process, it's important to select best-in-class districts that represent success. These districts can be used as exemplars as you begin to analyze your own data. They will help you to set meaningful, realistic goals for success as you begin improvement planning and UDL implementation.

Businesses have used the term *best-in-class* for decades to identify organizations that set the bar for success and deliver a greater value to consumers than competitors (Lacity & Willcocks, 2014). In a recent study of best-in-class businesses who provide business process outsourcing (BPO), the authors noted, "The best-in-class BPO relationships we studied helped clients implement shared services on a global scale, enabled rapid growth, delivered products to customers faster, and increased the bottom line by capturing more discounts and by reducing errors" (Lacity & Willcocks, 2014, p.131). If we view this research summary through an educational lens, we can see similarities between the goals of businesses and those of our educational institutions (Table 2.4).

Table 2.4: Crosswalk of best-in-class business and best-in-class education

Best-in-Class Business (Lacity & Willcocks, 2014, p. 131)	Best-in-Class Education
Help clients implement shared services on a global scale	Help students learn twenty-first-century skills to be competitive in a global marketplace
Enable rapid growth	Ensure equal growth between all students and student subgroups including low-income, students with disabilities, minority students, and English language learners
Deliver products to customers faster	Deliver effective services to students efficiently, using researched-based best practices
Increase the bottom line by capturing more discounts and by reducing errors	Increase the performance of all students by prioritizing educational spending and reducing or eliminating systems, structures, and practices that present barriers to improved student outcomes

If we further examine best practices of best-in-class businesses, we can highlight additional similarities between a business's bottom line, and our bottom line as educators—student learning.

Lacity and Willcocks (2014) present a table, "The Nine Practices for Best-in-Class BPO Performance." These nine practices (Table 2.5) are organized into three steps that align nicely to the work we seek to do as leaders. Best-in-class businesses must launch their mission, stay on target, and explore new frontiers. As educators, these nine practices offer connections to our work, as well. We have highlighted these patterns in Table 2.5.

Table 2.5: Similarities between best-in-class BPO performance and education

Practices for Best-in-Class BPO Performance (Adapted from Lacity & Willcocks, 2014)		Connection to Education
Launch the mission	**Assign great leaders.** Leaders "must work collaboratively to implement the practices associated with best-in-class performance" (p. 136).	As UDL leaders, we have to work collaboratively with all stakeholders to "launch our mission" or our improvement efforts. Fostering collaboration and community, and engaging multiple stakeholders, allows for a distributed model of leadership where numerous people are committed to increasing performance.
	Focus on business and strategic benefits beyond cost efficiencies. "These relationships focus on achieving more strategic benefits" (p. 137).	Our "cost efficiencies" are student achievement scores. True success in a district, however, goes beyond standardized data. We, as leaders, must examine multiple data sources to achieve more strategic benefits, such as student social-emotional health, reduced class sizes, and the incorporation of quality programming in all aspects of education including the arts, world language, and physical and behavioral health.
	Acquire strong transition and change-management capabilities. "Service excellence cannot happen without investing both in resources like onsite managers and in knowledge transfer (e.g., shadowing, mentoring and training)" (p. 138).	Once leaders identify best practices in best-in-class districts, and multiple stakeholders are invested in transitioning to the implementation of those practices, leaders must consider how to transfer the knowledge of those best practices into the district. Considerations such as sustained professional development are important as the "mission" is launched.

Table 2.5: Similarities between best-in-class BPO performance and education (continued)

Practices for Best-in-Class BPO Performance (Adapted from Lacity & Willcocks, 2014)		Connection to Education
Stay on target	**Adopt a partnering approach to governance.** "A partnering approach to governance is much more than a set of committees: it also comprises embedded partnership attitudes and behaviors" (p. 139).	We, as leaders, must remember that district growth requires more than just a set of committees and stakeholder buy-in. Once we identify the need for UDL implementation and district improvement, we must stay on target with an integrated and sustainable plan. This requires a shift in culture, so we must work to create a culture of improvement before trying to make large-scale changes.
	Align the retained organization with processes and the provider's staff. "Effective client leaders in charge of back offices build best-in-class retained organizations characterized by service excellence, low costs, scalability, flexibility, high compliance, and superior customer satisfaction (p. 140).	Staying on target is all about the whole team. Our "retained organization" is our community at large and so we need to work to provide excellent service, cost-effective improvements, and superior customer service, while aligning improvements with district policies, and state and federal laws. The UDL framework focuses on the importance of involving all stakeholders from the beginning to align the vision and the district improvement plan and improve our "customer satisfaction."
	Resolve issues and conflicts together and fairly. In these organizations, the business and the partnering organizations "seek to resolve issues together" (p. 141).	As stated previously, our districts serve our communities and so when we are confronted with problems that disrupt our performance, we must work together to identify the problems, set goals to address the problems and monitor our progress together.

Table 2.5: Similarities between best-in-class BPO performance and education (continued)

Practices for Best-in-Class BPO Performance (Adapted from Lacity & Willcocks, 2014)		Connection to Education
Explore new frontiers	**Use technology as an enabler and accelerator of performance.** "Best-in-class BPO relationships leverage technology for business outcomes" (p. 142).	The National Education Technology Plan, *Future Ready Learning: Reimagining the Role of Technology in Education* (U.S. Department of Education, 2016) calls for all education leaders to "develop a shared vision for how technology can support learning and how to secure appropriate resources to sustain technology initiatives. Leaders seek input from a diverse team of stakeholders to adopt and communicate clear goals for teaching, leading, and learning that are facilitated by technology. They model tolerance for risk and experimentation and create a culture of trust and innovation" (p. 40).
	Deploy expertise and business analytics. "In best-in-class relationships, the provider applies its domain expertise to launch rigorous analytics processes . . . to identify weaknesses and opportunities" (p. 143).	"Business analytics" or data analysis at the district level using multiple sources of evidence allows educational organizations to identify needs and opportunities for growth. A constant process of evidence-based decision-making allows the district to add value to their community.
	Prioritize and incentivize innovation. "Innovations are rarely realized because the provider's attention is focused on urgent operational issues" (p. 144).	So often, as leaders, our attention is focused on operational issues, but the research on best-in-class businesses communicates the need for an increased focus and commitment to innovation. As stated previously, this requires multiple stakeholders to be committed to this goal, so operational issues don't derail the goal to achieve greatness and increased outcomes for all students.

Just as businesses aim to provide a better consumer experience than competitors, school districts aim to provide the highest level of education to their students. When we, as leaders, identify districts who achieve at superior levels, we can examine their data and their practices to try to replicate their success. Once a district selects best-in-class districts and selects the data points to compare against, it's important to analyze and discuss this data with instructional data teams. We define instructional data teams as teams of educators working together to review data and discuss information as a means of increasing student or school success by informing, and thus improving, instructional practice, programs, and services.

With our administrative team, we engaged in a process to define a set of best-in-class districts and reviewed ourselves against these districts in regards to multiple factors in three categories: achievement and accountability data, enrollment and staffing data, and financial data. We used a simple ranking frequency method to determine the top-performing districts in our state, and used this list as our designation of best-in-class. We used a number of ranking lists, including 2014's "Best in Boston" (by *Boston* magazine) and the 2014 *Newsweek* top high schools. Your data team can examine local ranking and select the most valid measures in the area. Just be sure to select rankings that quantify variables, in addition to academic achievement. For example, "Best in Boston" looked at "test scores, student-to-teacher ratios, [and] graduation rates," while *Newsweek* took into consideration factors such as enrollment rates, graduation rates, standardized test scores, student attrition rates, and counselor-to-student ratios. One important thing to note is that some rankings depend on information sent from the district, and others simply do not include all districts. For example, "Best in Boston" includes "Only public schools within the Greater Boston I-495 boundary." Although our own district did not meet this criterion, we did include it in our best-in-class set of rankings.

Regardless of how you choose to define *best-in-class*, it's important to have exemplars for educational success, so you have measures to compare to your own data once it is collected and analyzed.

Determine and Articulate Weaknesses in Data Collection Methods

In determining the methods of data collection, parameters should be set and maintained during the planning stage. After selecting the data sources and identifying best-in-class districts, ensure that all types of knowledge are used.

If they are not, discuss why they aren't. At this stage, determine how these various sources of knowledge will be represented. Your team may find value in asking the following questions before discussing the limitations of certain data-collection methods. There are no correct or incorrect answers, but it's important to set goals for the quality and quantity of information and resources you will find to truly understand the strengths and weaknesses in the district.

- How much data is enough? Do we require a triangulation of data?
- What kind of data will be considered: quantitative? qualitative? mixed methods?
- What are the parameters for quality research? Will we accept online blogs and published dissertations, or are we limiting ourselves to peer-reviewed journals and studies published by well-known universities and tenured professors?
- What is our baseline for a trend? Is it three years? Five years? Ten years?
- What are the limitations of our collection methods?

The best way to illustrate this section is to share a product of practice. When we conducted a series of open forums, we needed to articulate the limitations of our data, however rich it was. See the sidebar "Qualitative Data Bias Acknowledgment" for a snapshot of a report from these open forums that discloses these limitations.

Identifying Themes in Data Collection

Once you have built a data culture, set norms, identified the data sources, and discussed the parameters for meaningful data, it's time to decide how you will analyze the data and determine themes. Thematically coding the data is an essential part of taking the multitude of information and narrowing the focus areas. The district must determine when in the process they wish to identify these themes. Some prefer to do it in the design phase. They articulate specific areas for research and data review prior to data collection. For example, a district may determine that it wants to align with state expectations, which may include anything from documents that articulate governing and regulatory practices to supplemental documents. Other districts may choose to determine the groups of knowledge collected (organizational, practitioner, user, research, policy) and identify data sources among those.

QUALITATIVE DATA BIAS ACKNOWLEDGEMENT

We need to acknowledge the following sample bias in our qualitative surveys and open forums.

Undercoverage.   This occurs when some groups are left out, or are significantly underrepresented in the sample. An example of this may be found if staff members participate in a paper-and-pencil survey and the results are analyzed for frequency to determine themes. Due to the smaller number of staff in certain departments, such as fine arts, counseling, or world language, their contributions may not result in a frequency large enough to be included in the analysis.

Nonresponse bias.   Sometimes, individuals chosen for the sample can't be contacted, or refuse to participate. An example of how this can happen is with the use of online surveys. For example, imagine that you wish to collect data on the community's priorities for your district. If you only send out the survey link electronically, you will miss a whole segment of stakeholders who aren't tech savvy. If you are only going to use an electronic method, be careful not to overgeneralize these results as fully representing the entire stakeholder group.

Voluntary response bias.   This occurs when sample members volunteer, so their willingness to participate may show bias, because people with strong opinions are more likely to offer a response. An example of this would be at an open forum where participants who feel very strongly (for or against) a particular topic of discussion, may be more likely to dominate the discussion.

Next, when analyzing the data, engage in thematic coding exercises to determine relevance in data under emerging themes. For example, we used a thematic coding protocol when interpreting data from each stakeholder open-forum session. Thematic coding is a form of qualitative analysis that involves identifying passages of text or images that are linked by a common theme to create categories. Charmaz (2003) suggests some basic questions to guide this work:

- What is going on?
- What is the person really saying?
- What do these actions and statements take for granted? (Think about motivation.)

This process is crucial to optimize relevance, value, and authenticity in all stakeholders.

Once all data is collected and analyzed, a set of triangulated data points will begin to form into themes and trends for necessary improvement. The community can engage in a process of problem statement identification from the various problems and themes. This process narrows down the generalized themes into ones that are specific and disaggregated. Before actually beginning the data-analysis process, determine a strategy for completing the work and also communicating the outcomes of the work.

Design the Framework to Communicate the Work

Here is a scenario that is likely familiar to you: You and your team members have been engaged in multiyear work, with broad constituent group participation. About eight months into the initiative, someone asks a staff member about it. He or she either claims not to know about it, or has no idea where the initiative came from. When this happens, you likely feel frustrated and defensive. We all do.

However, when this occurs, we really need to sit back and take stock and ownership over our messaging and communication. By prioritizing our work and focusing our outreach about this work, we can ensure a greater amount of communication and buy-in. One of our biggest mistakes after we create an initiative is that we forget to put the time into educating others about it. We need to create a communication plan for this important work. It must include two-way communication methods and result in high engagement in all stakeholders groups. We often rely too heavily on putting it on our website and assuming people will search for it.

In a 2011 Statewide Longitudinal Data Systems Best Practices brief titled *Stakeholder Communication: Tips from the States* (National Center for Education Statistics, 2011), a series of recommendations are given, including reaching out to stakeholders early in the process, and creating a carefully developed plan. In working with different stakeholders, it is essential to tailor the message. How you interact with students and staff may be very different from the audience at the local senior center.

Even methods of outreach vary according to stakeholder groups. We may have direct contact information for staff and parents, but how do we get the message out to those members of the community for whom we do not have an e-mail address? We have to be thoughtful about the desires of the community at large, and the distinct preferences of individual stakeholder groups. Do they prefer mailings, e-mails, blog posts, or social media outlets?

We have to be ready to offer multiple means of representation by posting the same information in multiple formats and for multiple audiences, and tailoring those messages for task, purpose, and audience. We must juxtapose traditional methods with more innovative methods that leverage technology. To harken back to the audience who is not going to seek information in an electronic format, there are often free resources we can use. For example, you may be able to share important district news press releases and letters to the editor in local papers. You could also seek to get airtime on local access cable programming, or collaborate with the town to send information in tax bills that are already being bulk mailed.

In creating your plan, be mindful of incorporating UDL practices. After all, it would be tragically ironic if your communication plan did not take into consideration the principles of UDL. Table 2.6 shows various communication methods and practices (adapted from the SLDS brief) and how they align with UDL principles. If you are interested in pursuing this concept in more depth, we will share more examples and a model communication plan in a forthcoming companion to this book.

Table 2.6: Communicating with Multiple Stakeholders Using UDL (Adapted from National Center for Education Statistics, 2011)

Multiple means of engagement	Multiple means of representation	Multiple means of action and expression
to stimulate motivation and interest	to present information and content in different ways	to differentiate the ways people share what they know
• Find and engage with a range of key stakeholders early in the process (and throughout it) and acknowledge their contributions. • Identify key stakeholders to serve as leaders of the project work or of specific parts of an initiative. • Utilize a group to help lead the outreach efforts, to define the work, to develop the communication plan, and to implement it.	• Understand the differences among various stakeholder groups and define the message to meet their needs and preferences. • Create a plan that is inclusive of multiple methods of communication (in person, online, including videos, photos, paper, podcasts, television appearances, newspaper articles, infographics, and so on). • Take away confusing jargon and acronyms from the messaging. Use language that is accessible to the general public.	• Create mechanisms for meetings around specific components of the work or plan to gather feedback and monitor progress in tandem with your change efforts. • Offer various methods and opportunities for ongoing feedback from key stakeholders (interactive forums, surveys, meetings with groups). • Define some early actions that can be implemented easily and successfully and share this information out.

As we shared in the beginning of this chapter, the Explore phase is critical to build a solid foundation for the need for UDL in your district. Following the aforementioned steps before preparing for UDL implementation will ensure that you are building engagement with all stakeholders. You are also well on your way to becoming a best-in-class district as you incorporate nine practices that will help you to build your organization in innovative ways.

3

Analyzing and Interpreting the Data for the Needs Assessment

In this chapter, we will continue to highlight the importance of a comprehensive needs assessment as a component of the Explore phase. We will share specific examples and protocols to support administrators as they link together information-gathering, district and school goals, and action-plan development. Among these are the use of a logic model to clarify key concerns and possible solutions.

Being a leader requires patience. We live in a world where our stakeholders expect results. If we return to our construction analogy, we are tasked with building an estate for our community. Everyone wants to see the final product, standing strong with character and curb appeal. That's our end goal. Knowing that we will be judged by the final construction, it's tempting to pick up some wood, a hammer, and a handful of nails and begin building. However, the foundation work is critical and cannot be rushed. As American songwriter David Allan Coe reminds us, "It is not the beauty of a building you should look at; it's the construction of the foundation that will stand the test of time." At this stage, our foundation is still incomplete.

The voices of stakeholders need to be heard when we identify strengths and challenges during the data-analysis process. Our report of findings should define these challenges in the format of clear problem statements that can be further explored. To identify these challenges, a necessary next step is for evidence to be analyzed to determine root causes. If we consider the leadership and learning matrix (Figure 2.1), this allows us to utilize the knowledge of antecedents in the formation of the planned work. Identifying these antecedents is challenging work. Although it is more about correlation than causation, the basis of this work is to understand the "why?" Knowing why builds engagement as you share how to make improvements to student outcomes.

Simply put, root-cause analysis is used to define the causes of the problem statements. There are several versions of root-cause protocols. These can be purchased in commercial books or found free on state education department websites such as the District Data Team Toolkit (Massachusetts Department of of Elementary and Secondary Education, 2015).

Depending on the scale of the team and task, the group may be small or may be significant in size. If the root causes are at a district level, we suggest opportunities for all district stakeholders to be involved. Begin by confirming that the identified root causes relate to the problem statement. For all those that they relate to, ask the group to put the identified causes into two piles: causes within their control and those outside their control. Factors outside their control (state mandates, for example) are not alterable variables, so do not warrant attention in this process, although it may be valuable for other district work.

Once you identify causes that relate to the problem statements and are within your control, we suggest you put them in three categories of leverage: high impact, moderate impact, and low impact. If the cause, for example, relates to the problem statement, and is within our control, but has limited impact on district work, it may not be meaningful to the scope of the plan. Those that are high-impact areas, are within our control, and are related to the problem statement should be moved to the next set of tasks.

The next set of tasks also needs to be built on the UDL foundation. A problem statement must be valuable and relevant to all stakeholders. For example, let's examine a problem that affects most districts in our nation. Imagine, based on multiple sources of evidence, you determine that your problem statement is that there is an achievement gap between special education students and general education students. You would then complete root-cause analysis and determine what potential root causes are within the locus of your control. Your next step is to determine whether or not the root causes are supported by all stakeholders. This is what we call the *validation component*, when we have to ensure that our three feedback triggers are minimized or eliminated. So, how do you do this work?

To build this engagement, all stakeholders must collaborate to validate these causes. This can be done through in-person workshops or mechanisms such as online surveys. When designing these validation exercises, provide multiple options, so stakeholders can review the data, the problem statement, and the potential root causes. Next, provide multiple means of expression so they have the opportunity to validate that, from their experience, they are in fact root causes of the problem. The trend of identified root causes across teams, grades, departments, and schools are then put through an additional process of verification. This may involve looking at additional data or reviewing research as a means to monitor progress and ensure continued engagement.

Take the above problem statement: there is an achievement gap between special education students and general education students. Based on the implementation of Multi-Tiered Systems of Support across the country, it is possible that during root-cause analysis, one potential root cause identified is the lack of a comprehensive, tiered instructional model in the district. This potential root cause could be validated in a few ways. The first is through a research review that demonstrates a correlation between tiered instructional models and student achievement. In addition, it could be validated by a survey of staff who indicate that there are limited or no staff present to support a tiered instructional model. Alternatively, the staff could note that they are not utilized to meet the needs of students who need Tier II support. In order to verify this, the district could conduct an analysis of staffing levels and schedules, past and present. If this analysis shows, for example, that there was clear evidence of a lack of essential staffing positions in Tier II (such as math specialists), the root cause of staffing would be verified. To verify this as a root cause related to student achievement gaps, performance of students who had the benefit of Tier II services could be compared with those who had not received these services but would have qualified. Results of these cohorts could be compared to demonstrate the correlation between the achievement gap and lack of Tier II supports. Once root causes have been identified, validated, and verified, you must communicate this information back to stakeholders so they are aware that the collaboration resulted in solid antecedents.

Once an evidence-based culture exists and professional development has occurred about how to examine, describe, and interpret data, and data has been analyzed for the identification of strengths and challenges, many districts ask, "Now what?" If we know what we do and why it works, we highlight these best practices for scaling up within our district. For those areas of challenge, we must prepare in order to guide appropriate goal-setting with the use of SMART goals, define a strategy to reach those goals, manage information and resources, and consistently monitor our progress.

In our role of leaders, we are tasked with building the foundation for our schools to flourish. A foundation alone, however, will not result in a high-performing district. It's the house that we build upon our foundation that will define us as leaders. If we reexamine Emerson's quote, we are reminded of the immense responsibility it is to manage a house. Once we build the foundation and the structure, we must "furnish, watch, show it, and keep it in repair, the rest of [our] days."

Thus far, we have discussed the importance of using the Explore phase, or the site work, to ready ourselves to pour our foundation. Once we are confident we have found the place to pour this foundation, we must also design our house. A strategy is similar to well-designed floor plans and MEP schematics (mechanical, electrical, plumbing designs). For those of us who aren't architects, those are two integral diagrams that communicate the design of the house to contractors, which allows them to turn the homeowner's vision into a reality.

Well-designed floor plans consider efficient use of space and strategic adjacencies. MEP schematics include the general layout of the system or the design intent of the mechanical, electrical, and plumbing systems so all of them are well-integrated and coordinated. Taken together, these diagrams create a strategic plan of action. So, how do we become architects in our district and design these plans? The work begins with the logic model.

What Is a Logic Model?

A *logic model*, in its most simple definition, is a tool to plan, implement, and evaluate district improvement strategies and initiatives (Curtis and City, 2009; Shakman & Rodriguez, 2015). Frechtling (2007) defines the concept of a logic model as a tool to describe the theory of change underlying an intervention. She describes the connections between the concept of logic model and program-theory evaluation in that they both make underlying assumptions of the change explicit, and define the link between the actions of the plan (project) and goal attainment. While the logic model concept was not generated especially for educational pursuits, it fits well into our framework for change.

Kekahio, Cicchinelli, Lawton, and Brandon (2014) write that the logic model has many benefits, such as helping to guide our work, define evaluation questions, and form well-articulated and actionable evaluation questions. In other words, the logic model puts the plan out on the table: it draws a direct correlation to what we think will happen and how we will know if it was successful. In the process of defining a district strategy, the logic model forces us to be overt about our work. It makes us be clear about what actions we are taking, how we will measure our success, and what assumptions underlie the work.

The National Center for Education Evaluation and Regional Assistance (2015) lists the logic model's benefits this way:

- Brings detail to broad goals;
- Helps identify gaps in program logic and clarify assumptions;
- Builds understanding and promotes consensus;
- Makes explicit underlying beliefs;
- Helps clarify *what* is appropriate to evaluate—and *when*; and
- Summarizes complex programs for effective communication.

In the model shared by Curtis and City (2009), you create an overall strategy that includes a theory of action that leads to the development of strategic objectives and initiatives. In their logic model sequence, they encourage planned work (activities and resources) to lead to intended results (outputs, outcomes, and measures), coupled with reasoning measures (checking our assumptions).

Regardless of defined steps in different versions of the model, the intent is the same. We know we have a challenge and know where we are; we also have an idea of where we want to be. The logic model helps us to define how are we going to get from the idea to a fully drafted home, and how will we monitor progress to know we are going in the correct direction. No matter the format, the logic model has, in its most basic form, four components.

In a review of program evaluation models and with reliance on Frechtling (2007), Frye and Hemmer (2012) define the four main components of a simple logic model as: inputs, activities, outputs, and outcomes. The inputs include variables that districts contribute to the work. They may include tangible items such as instructional materials, or intangible items such as time for teams to meet. Activities are actions based on strategies. They list the programmatic changes that will occur. Kekahio, Cicchinelli, Lawton, and Brandon (2014) describe them as the processes, actions, and events that will occur.

The outputs are the product of the activities. They answer the question, "What has changed?" They are tangible and can be defined as process- or product-based. Process outputs can be that a series of professional development sessions have occurred and a product outputs can be the sign-in sheet showing how many participants attended. The outputs represent the results of these changes and can be short-term, medium-term, and long-term. To identify outcomes, you may ask yourself: "What did the teachers learn in those professional development sessions (PD evaluation form results)?", "What changes to their practices occurred (observational data)?", and "How did it impact student learning (student assessment results)?"

The logic model is usually constructed as a map with arrows going from inputs to activities, to outputs to outcomes (Figure 3.1).

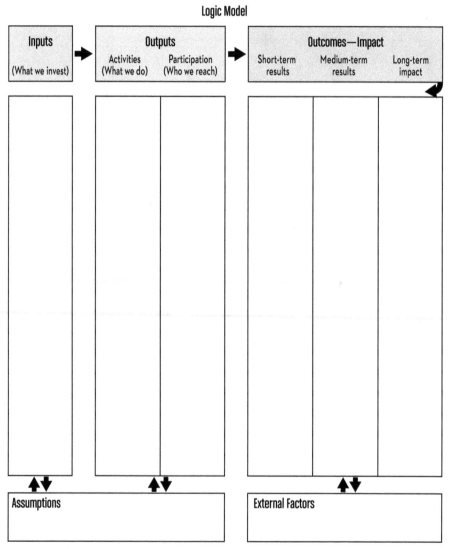

Figure 3.1: Logic model template (adapted from University of Wisconsin-Extension, Program Development and Evaluation, 2002).

A District Example

Let's deconstruct the logic model with an example. Imagine we identify a growing achievement gap between our special education and general education students in their math proficiency scores, as defined by state and local assessments. We identify the specific data sets to target the problem, conduct research, and engage in root-cause analysis. We know our baseline and then create a strategy with defined objectives. Going back to the schematics analogy, we become the architects in this phase. We are mapping out what goes where and drafting the picture of our plan. This plan takes the realized house (the met objectives) and the reality of the work site (challenge statement) and begins to construct an architectural draft of the home.

The needs assessment should identify a problem statement and the antecedents through root-cause analysis. For example, in the section above, we identified a problem statement of an achievement gap between special education and general education students. The root-cause analysis identified, validated, and verified one root cause as the lack of math specialists to provide Tier II support. In the needs assessment, you can analyze this against multiple measures of data. For example, over a five-year period, and on multiple measures, do you see an achievement gap between your special education subgroup and general education students at multiple levels or within multiple schools? If so, you can create an objective that serves as a reflection of where you want to be: *Within two years, the achievement gap for students with disabilities versus general education students will be decreased by 10 points, as measured by the state accountability report.* Under the objectives lie sets of initiatives that are developed by the root-cause analysis exercise. Each initiative will have an articulated plan inclusive of the inputs, activities, outputs, and outcomes.

This logic model provides a strategic bridge from where we are to where we want to be. It helps us monitor our progress through self-assessment and reflection to determine the impact our initiatives are having on our students. The logic model is not the same as an action plan, which needs to be developed from the logic model, and does not tell you *who* is doing *what* and *when* are they doing it. But the logic model will be essential in taking that next step: constructing the action plan itself by defining what is happening between the challenge (problem statement) and the goal. In other words, you can use the components of the logic model and paste them into existing district action-plan templates.

Assuming the problem statement above, one of the inputs, or resources, would be to hire math specialists to provide Tier II support. This would allow the necessary scaffolding and support at the appropriate level, serve as a resource to Tier I staff, and eventually reduce the overburdened caseload of special educators.

Activities for this resource included hiring math specialists, providing ongoing PD and support for them, defining criteria for entrance and exit of said services, defining the model of delivery, and purchasing curriculum resources to support their students. An example of a defined output for this example would be that each elementary school would hire a math specialist for grades K–1 and another for grades 2–4.

The short-term outcome could be defined by viewing growth between diagnostic and mid-process scores on progress-monitoring tools. Long-term outcomes could be defined by progress on state scores and accountability ratings in demonstrating growth of this sub-group's scores. The problem statement was much more complex than this one resource, but as you can see from this example, the model provides support as you examine each activity.

What Does a UDL-based Logic Model Look Like?

For so many years, we created plans based on the actions of adults and not the outcomes of our students. We had action steps about professional development, and the success measures were defined by us completing the task. We never asked ourselves whether it had any meaningful impact on achievement. Logic models hold us accountable for student outcomes. They provide information that can be fleshed out into a comprehensive strategy with defined timeframes, tracked measures, and identified staff responsible for the work.

Often, we define action plans within the context of what we, as adults, do. We measure progress by how many staff took a PD session. We rarely track whether the PD had a positive correlation with student performance. The logic model forces us to view our success in terms of our action's impact on staff and students.

Table 3.1 shows an articulated strategic objective and logic model sequence. We used our district's work to implement UDL as a district-wide framework as an example to model how the sequence works. From this example, you will see the principles of the logic model sequence as we worked to develop an awareness and understanding of UDL, implement UDL authentically in the classroom, and raise student achievement while closing achievement gaps.

Table 3.1: Logic model alignment to district work on UDL

Sample Problem Statement	There is an achievement gap between special education and general education students. This has been supported by a five-year trend of data on multiple measures.
Strategic Objective	The district will create a Multi-Tiered System of Support (MTSS) model, inclusive of standards-based instruction and assessment, Universal Design for Learning (UDL), and Positive Behavioral Interventions and Supports (PBIS).
Initiative	Train a cohort of teachers and leaders in UDL, who will serve as a task force to plan for future full-district implementation of UDL.

Table 3.2 is a sample logic model for one of initiatives based on a verified and validated root cause, which was that our educators had never had any professional development in UDL. Other high-impact root causes would also need to be addressed with additional initiatives.

How you apply the logic model to your district depends on a few factors. Before you utilize the logic model, a few foundational components need to be in place. We spent a whole chapter on the concept of information-based decision-making. The data needed for that concept is an essential component of the outcomes section of your logic model. Once you have systems to thoughtfully review data, set goals, and define potential root causes, the development of the logic model is a natural extension. You take the data and determine a SMART goal. Then, you take the verified and validated root causes and use those to define the resources and action steps necessary. You build the logic model to be meaningful not only in the work you do, but also in how you will measure your success.

All of this work—building a culture of evidence-based decision-making that eliminates the three feedback triggers, engaging in root-cause analysis, and engaging in the logic model and goal-setting process—is necessary for all stakeholders to become resourceful, strategic, and purposeful participants in our district's improvement efforts. Once you have completed research on UDL, the needs of your district, and your vision moving forward, you are finished with the Explore phase and it's time to start preparing. The site work is done; your blueprints are in hand. You are ready to build a palace.

Table 3.2: Logic model example based on the root cause of no UDL professional development

| Activities
What Will Be Done? | Resources
What Is Needed to Help Get the Work Done? | Outputs
What Is the Result of the Activity? | Outcomes
What Impact Will the Outputs Have on Our Organization? | Measures
How Will We Assess This Impact? | Assumptions
What Are We Taking for Granted in Our Model? |
|---|---|---|---|---|---|
| Offer three-credit, graduate-level course in UDL for educators | Obtain well-qualified instructor and ensure access to appropriate space, materials, and technology

Obtain a contract with a local university to offer the course in-house | 25 staff members complete the course

Sample projects and lessons shared | Staff from this class will begin implementing UDL principles into their lesson design and assessment practices.

Staff will have practical experience that they can use when designing the UDL district model.

Sample lessons and assessments will be available as exemplars for power elements of the district's evaluation rubrics. | Observations of staff who participated, using UDL: "look-fors"

Evaluation forms for the course, where staff articulate the impact the class will have on their practice

Review student achievement data of participants | The educators will believe that UDL will successfully help us close the achievement gap by understanding the research and reviewing the root-cause analysis.

The staff who participate in this class will attend regularly and participate fully in the class, will buy into the principles of UDL, and will implement what they learned with fidelity. |

Table 3.2: Logic model example based on the problem of no UDL professional development (continued)

Activities *What Will Be Done?*	Resources *What Is Needed to Help Get the Work Done?*	Outputs *What Is the Result of the Activity?*	Outcomes *What Impact Will the Outputs Have on Our Organization?*	Measures *How Will We Assess This Impact?*	Assumptions *What Are We Taking for Granted in Our Model?*
Offer three-credit, graduate-level course on UDL for administrators	Obtain a well-qualified instructor and ensure access to appropriate space, materials, and technology Obtain a contract with a local university to offer the course in-house.	15 administrators complete the course Sample universally designed artifacts (meeting agendas) and observational feedback shared	Administrators will begin to implement this knowledge in their practice. Observations will incorporate UDL look-fors (when applicable) and at least 50 percent of their meetings and work products will be universally designed. Administrators will have practical experience that they can use when designing the UDL district model.	Observations and artifacts of practice for administrators to demonstrate universally designed practice in their leadership Evaluation forms for the course where staff articulate the impact the class will have on their practice Review survey data of staff about administrative practices	The administrators will believe that UDL will successfully help us close the achievement gap by understanding the research and reviewing the root-cause analysis. The administrators who participate in this class will attend regularly and participate fully in the class, will buy into the principles of UDL, and will implement what they learned with fidelity.

Table 3.2: Logic model example based on the problem of no UDL professional development (continued)

Activities *What Will Be Done?*	Resources *What Is Needed to Help Get the Work Done?*	Outputs *What Is the Result of the Activity?*	Outcomes *What Impact Will the Outputs Have on Our Organization?*	Measures *How Will We Assess This Impact?*	Assumptions *What Are We Taking for Granted in Our Model?*
Develop a UDL task force (a sub-committee of the wider MTSS district working group) who will create a model and plan for UDL implementation districtwide	Guidebook on UDL Implementation Phases Time and stipends or coverage money for participants in committee to meet Ensure access to appropriate space, materials, and technology	A completed multi-year plan for the UDL phases of Explore, Prepare, and Integrate that is shared with the community	The plan will map needed resources and processes (i.e., specific personnel, structures such as planning time, materials, curriculum, and professional development). The plan will define a strategic vision, plan of action, and expected outcomes.	The plan will be assessed against a defined plan development rubric, including processes completed, and the incorporation of vision, activity completion, and defined outcomes.	If a plan is developed, the district will align resources to allow the plan to be implemented. The district will focus on the plan in order to allow the staff to concentrate on this work and not be distracted by too many other initiatives.
Create a set of video segments on UDL practice in the district to be shared with the staff and community to build engagement	Camera for filming Editing equipment, staff expertise, and time to develop video segments Digital library storage area	A series of five videos explaining UDL and showing what it looks like in our district Local TV show dedicated to segments on UDL aired	The staff and community will watch the videos and learn about what UDL is and what it looks like in practice.	Surveys of staff attitudes and understanding of UDL before and after the video series A review of analytics for the videos to see how many people viewed it in the community	Once the staff and community understand what UDL is, they will be more willing to provide resources to support the required staffing and PD necessary.

If, during the Explore phase, we try to move ahead with district improvement without using an evidence-based decision-making approach grounded in UDL, we will likely remember those fateful words from *This Old House*: "Neglect even one of these, and the most carefully poured foundation can fail."

4

UDL and Strategic Thinking

This chapter will introduce the Prepare phase of UDL implementation by discussing how to create a culture that is flexible and maintains high expectations for all, and how to define a strategic vision that is aided by UDL. Specific focus will be on examining and refining district vision and strategy through the UDL lens, using UDL as a tool to achieve district improvement goals and strategy, and providing examples of how to be thoughtful and purposeful in strategic planning with all stakeholders to increase district-wide engagement and foster collaboration and community.

We, as leaders, have the power to inspire and improve every aspect of operation in our organizations. When our districts and schools flourish, we do not take the credit. When things fall apart, we take the blame. That's the magic of being a leader, but it's also our Achilles' heel. If you need a little refresher on Greek mythology, Achilles was just a sweet little baby when his mother was told that her son would die young. Of course, she, as any mother would, trekked to the River of Styx, where the waters promised invincibility. To protect her son, she held him by the heel and dipped him in that water, coating him with an armor of power. Unfortunately, there was one spot the magical waters could not protect—the heel. Fast-forward many years, and Achilles was fighting in a war. One poisonous arrow was shot and stuck in his heel. That was his downfall.

When planning for UDL implementation, we must prepare so we do not leave even one area of weakness. We must get every stakeholder involved and we must hold everyone to high expectations. If we do not, a poisonous arrow could come at any time, we will have to take the blame, and that could set back UDL implementation in our district.

So, how do we create a culture where everyone is prepared to implement an integrated and sustainable model of UDL? Most importantly, as we begin the

Prepare phase, we must model the UDL framework and provide options for our stakeholders to build executive function and self-regulation strategies. If we do not focus on these Guidelines during this phase, we will not have the necessary foundation to build a culture where high expectations and a growth mindset are the norm.

Once we share the needs assessment, we know *why* we need to continue to implement UDL as a district-wide tool, and we know *what* barriers we need to overcome to realize our vision and true potential. The next step is to develop the district strategy, or *how* we're going to get there. In order to do that, we need to continue to foster collaboration and community with all stakeholders. We need to embrace our communities and encourage them to hold us to high expectations as we design a strategy that holds all students, regardless of variability, to the highest of expectations. This strategy will act as a road map that will allow us to eliminate detours and barriers so we can realize the true potential. To do this, our districts need a vision.

Creating a vision is no easy task, but having one is vital for the success of your organization. Think of a well-articulated vision as a guidepost for years to come. We, as leaders, must put the necessary time, energy, and resources into it that it deserves. Whether you do this work within the district, or utilize a consultant, there are best practices that will make the whole process smooth.

Our district chose to have a facilitator come in to guide our vision work so key stakeholders could be full participants and not relegated to the facilitator role. We used the Future Search Network model (Weisbord & Janoff, 2016) to guide our work. A Future Search is a model that encourages collaboration and community from various stakeholders—that is, "those with resources, expertise, formal authority, and need"—in order to discover common ground and create a vision that spurs shared action (Weisbord & Janoff, 2016).

In our district, this particular model was intended to create a shared vision that would lead to a long-range strategy. We participated in a one-and-a-half-day retreat focused on the four key principles of the future search design, which include:

- gathering all stakeholders,
- defining the global context of the work,
- focusing our work on the future, and
- engaging in self-management and action.

We aligned with the four key principles by first engaging a wide spectrum of stakeholders to represent the full community. We identified various stakeholders, and then our vision planning team sent out over 200 personal invitations to key stakeholders by making phone calls and sending handwritten letters. We also sent out invitations to all members of the community using multiple means of representation (press releases and announcements at public meetings, for example). These methods resulted in over 80 participants from various stakeholders groups.

During the retreat, we engaged in the exploration of the "global content" for our work. We discussed our history in terms of local, state, and national issues that impacted our schools. Next, we examined our current state. We identified what was working and what we need to focus on for improvement. We then shifted toward a vision for the future, with a focus on common ground. The outcomes of this retreat built the foundation of our vision, mission, and core values, and created a direction for our future strategic planning.

Of course, creating a vision is not a means to an end. Once you create your vision, you'll want to consistently invite mastery-oriented feedback to continue to hold your organization to the high expectations you set forth when your strategy was being developed. Once your vision is tailored for your organization, you have to ensure you have a culture where feedback is valued so all stakeholders are able to persevere as they work toward intended outcomes in the strategy.

Feedback as a Strategy Tool

A culture of high expectations is one where feedback is encouraged, analyzed, communicated, and utilized to make important decisions. Accepting feedback, however, is both an art and a science. If we want our organizations to thrive on meaningful feedback that ensures everyone is held to high standards, we need to change our culture. Again, this step is not optional. If this work is not done, your district's heel is exposed.

Stone and Heen (2014) explain that there are three types of feedback: appreciation, coaching, and evaluation. All three types of feedback have their place as we prepare for UDL implementation, but it is important that we understand how they are different, and which UDL Guidelines they align to, so we can ensure all stakeholders are committed to continued improvement and high standards. This work needs to be done before building the district strategy, because if all stakeholders aren't receptive to meaningful feedback, the vision and the plan will only be able to accomplish so much.

Appreciation is feedback about what we are doing well. In any job, it's great to hear words of affirmation, since this helps to improve culture. And let's face it: it makes people feel good. It's important, however, to create an environment where only real achievement and hard work are celebrated. Appreciating and celebrating mediocrity will get you—you guessed it—more mediocrity.

Although appreciation makes people feel good, it does little to actually improve performance. Imagine you walk into a fourth-grade co-taught classroom, and you see two teachers who are implementing a UDL lesson. You also know that these teachers consistently achieve significant student growth on both standardized and district measures in math and reading. On this day, students are learning about the state of Vermont in activities of their choosing. Some students are reading sections of their textbook on the state; others are gathered around the teacher, listening to a short presentation and viewing a Prezi; others are exploring travel brochures about Killington Mountain, the Vermont State House, the Ethan Allen Homestead, and the village of Woodstock. When they are finished, they can express their knowledge by recording a tourism commercial, writing a letter, giving an oral presentation, or creating their own brochure. Students are engaged and you are impressed, so you provide feedback about the quality of the lesson. In this scenario, appreciation is warranted; but often, the same appreciation will be given to the teacher down the hall who is teaching straight from an outdated textbook while students sit quietly in rows. This appreciation may be given even without evidence that the teacher is effective in increasing student outcomes. If both individuals receive appreciation, it will only maintain the status quo. Both will feel good about their practice and continue to do what they are doing. The problem is that one of the teachers does not personalize learning and will therefore not meet the needs of all students. Although both would improve with mastery-oriented feedback, it's critical when the district's high expectations for inclusive learning are clearly not being met.

If you examine your school or district's staff evaluations, you will likely see what we see in Massachusetts. For the 2013–2014 school year, 71,765 educators were evaluated; 86.5 percent of them were rated as proficient, while only 8.1 percent were exemplary (MA DESE, 2015b). Here's the problem: of the 8.1 percent of educators who were identified as being exemplary, only 32 percent of them achieved high student growth. Note that growth is not standardized achievement, nor does it reflect student ability. Student growth is the essence of what it means to be a teacher: did students grow in relationship to their peers over time? What is more upsetting is that close to 10 percent of these "exemplary" teachers actually saw low student growth. If our feedback is that teachers without high student outcomes are exemplary, then we are not holding our staff to high expectations.

So why do we give appreciation? Because it's necessary at times to help build self-regulation strategies. The UDL checkpoints remind us to promote expectations and beliefs that optimize motivation and facilitate coping skills and strategies. To do this, we have to provide appreciation when it is due. But we cannot stop there. We cannot define exemplary by low student growth. If we do, we have exposed our Achilles' heel.

When you read your staff evaluations, or even your own evaluation, you will likely read a lot of feedback that qualifies as appreciation. But appreciation only goes so far. If we want people to improve, we have to provide the second kind of feedback: *coaching*.

Coaching is about providing strategies to help all stakeholders work toward the high expectations we have for them. In UDL, we call this *mastery-oriented feedback*. We need to tell our stakeholders what they can do to improve, and we must allow our stakeholders to give us this feedback, as well. If we want our staff, our students, and our parents to be receptive to coaching feedback, we have to be, too. We can do this by actively seeking coaching feedback from our learning communities, analyzing that feedback, and then communicating it back out. When we do this, we must also model the importance of executive function. To be strategic learners, individuals must be able to guide appropriate goal-setting, create a strategy, manage resources to achieve that strategy, and consistently monitor progress, seek additional feedback, and adjust the strategy as necessary. This requires self-reflection and the ability to be open to the feedback that will allow us to improve.

If we think back to our classroom observation of our fourth-grade co-taught classroom, we could provide both appreciation and coaching. We have to create a culture where everyone expects to receive suggestions on how to improve. Yes, the lesson was universally designed; yes, students were engaged. But we can always find something to help push our stakeholders to the next level. We can commend performance, but we can follow-up with some coaching feedback such as, "When students begin to express their knowledge using the choice assignment, it would be beneficial for them to have multiple scaffolds so they can all work independently. If you haven't already, you may want to create exemplars and provide rubrics so all students know what a high-quality project will look like." Coaching feedback, like the previous statement, is often misconstrued as being the third type of feedback: *evaluation*.

Evaluation feedback is intended to aid in self-reflection and provide an objective view of where we stand. However, the delivery and reception of evaluation feedback can be tricky. It is often received as off-base, unfair, or poorly delivered (Stone & Heen, 2014). If the receiver of feedback believes an evaluation to be any or all of these things, the feedback is often discarded, and the truth triggers discussed in the previous chapter are activated. The danger is that often there is a way to find some truth by examining where the feedback is coming from and where it is going; by discarding the feedback, an individual is missing an opportunity to grow. The same is true with our districts. A part of building a culture of improvement is scaffolding the skills necessary to receive coaching and evaluation feedback well. Most importantly, we want to teach our stakeholders to expect it. We do this by owning *our* weaknesses in our needs assessment, encouraging feedback, and then reflecting publically on how the feedback will improve future goal-setting and strategy.

Last year, we began this work in our district by creating a Central Office Report Card. After teachers posted their grades for students, we created a Google Form and asked all our staff members to assign grades and provide comments about all central office administrators and their ability to effectively communicate and act as a professional resource, and their visibility in the district. When analyzing the comments, we received all three types of feedback. The appreciation was easy to read. The coaching and negative evaluations were not. Still, we persevered. We all analyzed our own data, identified trends, and set goals for our improvement with specific strategies. We then communicated these results to our teachers, because we felt it was crucial to model the value of feedback in improving our district's effectiveness.

Applying UDL Principles to Strategy Development

The principles of UDL need to be a component of strategy development. Let's take a moment to reflect on those principles. If we consider multiple means of representation, we have to ask ourselves, are we representing our newly formed vision, our needs-assessment data, our findings, and our SMART goals in a way that allows our community different ways to access and comprehend the information we provide? Actively ask if you are customizing the display of information. Are you using various forms of media and considering the benefits of presenting information with visual and auditory media (e.g., electronic, in-person, video)? Are your products tailored to certain stakeholders (e.g., by removing educational jargon when sharing materials with the greater community)? If necessary, provide important background language and vocabulary.

Once the needs assessment is shared and feedback is gathered, it is time to provide multiple means of action and expression. This is where strategy development comes into play, as a district strategy aligns to collective executive function. Here the Guidelines' emphasis on scaffolding the development of goals and plans can help.

There is often great variability within an administrative team or committee around the development of a district strategy. We often see that, rather than engage multiple stakeholders in the work, school leaders will just do the work themselves in isolation and bring it back to the committee or team for "review." This leads to exhausted leaders and a team that is not invested in the work. The energy needs to be put forth up front in developing the team's or committee's capacity to understand and share in the work of strategy development, perhaps through development training, exemplar development, tools for communication, and so forth. The upfront work will pay off in a shared commitment to the development of the strategy and in the basis of shared commitment to the plan.

Once the outcomes of the data analysis are shared in the needs assessment, and feedback is gathered, it is imperative to offer support in the development of sound strategy. One way is to use multiple tools for construction and composition when constructing the artifacts of strategy work (e.g., the report of findings, the vision statement, the core values). Similar to work we might do with students (such as providing access to spell-checker or text-to-speech software to remove barriers), provide opportunities for the group working on developing the strategy to access resources and means of collaboration (such as Google Docs or Skype) to take away barriers to the creation of work that may be impeded by busy schedules of committee members. When the products are completed, actively create forums and mechanisms to garner feedback about the draft strategy documents. If you have an open Google Doc, members can actively question and comment on draft components.

When working with the greater community, one example is to provide open forums or attend existing community meetings where you share draft documents and engage in a discussion about the artifacts. Another idea is to create online videos that explain the development of the document, and then provide opportunities for feedback such as an online form or an e-mail address. Another option is to share draft artifacts with people through e-mail and online posts and create mechanisms for directed feedback such as a structured online survey. As the work grows, people's institutional memory may fail them and they may not remember all the work that was done. It is an important component of strategy to offer external organizational aids to the community. Perhaps you can create a presentation or a timeline of the work to date, with links to the existing documents.

Lastly, take into consideration the work on feedback. Learning and growth cannot happen without feedback. Use the mechanisms for outreach and feedback, and listen actively. Adjust when necessary and articulate how feedback was considered and the outcomes that came from it.

This work is contingent on garnering community input on strategy development. This requires time and energy from members of your community. One way to help get your community involved in this work is to provide multiple means of engagement.

Individuals engage in work when they find it relevant and it is valuable to things they are interested in. Who isn't interested in the schools? To some degree, everyone in our community has some relationship with the schools in town. They either attended the schools, have their children in the schools, or had their children attend the schools. However, depending on how far removed they are from the schools, community members may not feel a great sense of engagement with them.

We need to work with all community members to help them understand our schools, find value in the schools, and ultimately to support them. The importance of community engagement may make them more willing to support the school financially, but it has much deeper meaning. Lopez and Caspe (2014) note that the concept of family and community engagement transcends two-way communication about student learning or the support that families can provide students. Their definition aligns to the UDL framework as they note the shared responsibility for districts and communities in connecting students to learning opportunities and connecting community resources to all students and families.

Just as strategic, goal-directed learners need executive-function skills to achieve at high levels, our schools, districts, and our communities need executive-function skills to become great. The UDL checkpoints remind us to guide appropriate goal-setting, create a strategy, and consistently monitor our progress, so we must develop the same framework for our school or district. This executive function is communicated in a district strategy. The needs assessment and the vision guide the setting of goals, but to monitor the progress of the strategy implementation, there must be consistent opportunities to collect all three types of feedback to ensure that we are not veering off the path to greatness and settling with proficient, when we could be exemplary. And, let's be clear: to be exemplary, we must have high levels of student growth for all students, regardless of variability, so every strategy needs to build its foundation on the pillars of UDL and student learning.

5

An Integrated District Strategy

Throughout this chapter, we will discuss the Prepare phase, specifically methods for districts to integrate UDL strategy into district, school, and educator goals as a means to monitor progress. Aligning all district improvement efforts to address the district's needs is critical as you prepare for implementation. By doing this in a vacuum, you may potentially allow for implementation fatigue or implementation gaps. The chapter includes examples of how districts integrated their UDL work into a greater district strategy. Lastly, we will provide guidance in how to integrate UDL into technology and capital planning.

In order for UDL to have enough life to grow, it must have constant attention and nourishment. This can be accomplished by making it a focus of all a district does. It makes sense to incorporate UDL into the overall district strategy, have schools and educators develop goals that support this district focus, and have accompanying plans (e.g., capital and technology plans) that support this work, as well.

There are many models a district may employ in developing its long-range work focused on improvement. Among other names, some call it a *long-range plan*, some a *strategic plan*, some an *improvement plan*, and some a *district strategy* (our choice). The concept is not new, but has been refined over recent years. We recommend that a district strategy be driven by a comprehensive needs assessment and a clearly articulated vision. It is the road map to go from where we are to where we want to be, and defines what will be accomplished in the confines of predetermined dates (three years, five years, and so on). Curtis and City (2009) encourage a district to focus its strategy on the *instructional core*—that is, what happens between an instructor and student in the presence of content.

By focusing on the instructional core and its student outcomes, and by forcing ourselves to target our work (three to five main objectives), we allow for a depth of work to be covered. We also avoid initiative overload, where we take on too many things to do any of them well. The district strategy should be driven by the needs assessment and the vision. By having a comprehensive needs assessment, we know what the most pressing issues are and by having a community-based vision, we know what things the community cares about and is excited and willing to provide support. No matter the structure you choose to develop in your strategy, it must be meaningful.

Choose objectives and goals that are data-driven and high-leverage, scaled appropriately for the time-bound nature of the plan, aligned with the mission and core values of the district, represent the community's needs, and drive the district closer to its ultimate vision for education. By engaging in the logic model, it is often easy to apply the contents of that work to a strategy action plan. The SMART goals are written, followed by related activities (action steps), outputs are defined, and outcomes are articulated.

What does this look like in practice? The Danvers Public Schools in Massachusetts created an overall district strategy that incorporated UDL. The district's K–12 curriculum director, Mary Wermers, explains: "We are not involved in an exclusive 'UDL initiative' but rather, we've studied the theories of UDL and incorporate strategies from the matrix into our curriculum, instruction, and assessment work. Much of the work is documented in the form of strategies and actions in our school or department logic models." By using UDL as a foundation for district improvement, districts can implement the framework in a meaningful and sustainable way without introducing a "new initiative" that may come and go.

One of Danvers's defined action steps was "K–12 teachers will apply Universal Design for Learning (UDL) principles and Skillful Teaching (ST) strategies in curriculum alignment to the Common Core and in developing well-structured lessons as part of their standards-based units." This was part of a strategic plan that spanned from 2013–2018. A mid-cycle report of the plan noted: "UDL strategies were highlighted at the October and January District Data Leadership Team Meetings with a focus on using UDL principles as instructional strategies in the school logic models. The following are the instructional strategies aligned to the UDL Guidelines that are documents in the individual school logic models." Table 5.1 shows examples from two Danvers schools.

Table 5.1: Danvers Schools' instructional strategies (used with permission)

School	
Thorpe	Teachers will develop an understanding of the principle #2 of UDL, Provide Multiple Means of Action and Expression, and apply UDL principles #1 and #2 to the design and implementation of lessons. • Teachers will provide explicit instruction using exemplars for quality constructed responses. • Teachers will model usage of a graphic organizer with gradual release. • Teachers will continue to have students develop close reading strategies for fiction and nonfiction texts in which all areas of Bloom's Taxonomy are incorporated. • Teachers will engage students in peer feedback (reference exemplars) and self-reflection to deepen their constructed responses.
HRMS	Teachers will incorporate the MA [Massachusetts] Common Core literacy standards across disciplines to aid in the implementation of the Guidelines and principles of Universal Design for Learning (UDL). • Teachers will model close reading strategy. • Teachers will support the use of and gradual release of a problem-solving template. • Teachers will provide opportunities for practicing problem-solving strategies. • Teachers will support student identification and application of relevant evidence through the use of "three read" and "stop and think" strategies to monitor comprehension, guided practice, and collaborative student discussion groups. • Teachers will support analysis of evidence to formulate interpretation of a complex text through the use of "three read" and "stop and think" strategies to monitor comprehension, guided practice, and collaborative student discussion groups. • Teachers will model the above strategies and provide feedback to students on how to improve.

The UDL Guidelines remind us that in order to build a district's executive function, we must guide appropriate goal-setting, support strategy development, manage information and resources, and enhance capacity to monitor progress. This process starts with the district strategy, but it is also important to align all systems to the strategy. In a previous chapter, we discussed the importance of MEP schematics when designing a house so all systems are integrated. In theory, three different architects could design mechanical plans, electrical plans, and plumbing plans, but that would not ensure efficiency or coordination. The same is true with a district's strategy, capital improvement plan (CIP), and technology plan.

A CIP is a link between an organization's vision and its annual capital expenditure budgets that is developed within the context of the larger strategic plan (Torma, 2015). The CIP process is similar to the process outlined in building the district's strategy, because it needs to involve engagement from all stakeholders (Table 5.2).

Table 5.2: Universally designing a capital improvement plan

Questions to Ask When Building a CIP (Adapted from Torma, 2015)

- Does the project appear in the district's comprehensive strategy?
- Is the project well thought out? Have feasibility studies on alternatives been adequate?
- Do the estimates of the projects seem reasonable based on contractors' bids for similar projects in the area?
- Is the project related to other projects? Is the sequence of construction reasonable?
- Is there a good balance between repair and maintenance and installation of new improvements?
- Are we spending enough on capital projects in comparison with annual operating expenses?

A technology plan is also a critical aspect of a district's larger UDL strategy. Managing technology requires a strategy of its own, which aligns with the district's vision and larger strategy. The following considerations, outlined in a research study on the effectiveness of strategic planning on the management of technology, should be examined when planning a technology strategy (Table 5.3). These considerations, although gleaned from research on technology planning in industry, have significant implications for education.

Table 5.3: Universally designing a district technology plan (adapted from Roy & Singh, 2015)

Expert Views on Strategic Technology Planning	Implications for Universally Designed Leadership in Education
Pillars of marketing are product, price, and publicity.	Technology plans must consider the value of technology and its ability to improve instructional and student outcomes, the potential cost of technology purchases, and how we will ensure effective rollout of the technology with a public relations campaign that provides information on how the technology will improve teaching and learning. • Guide appropriate goal-setting • Support planning and strategy development • Heighten salience of goals and objectives • Foster collaboration and community • Promote expectations and beliefs that optimize motivation
Customer education is an important element for business. Top management should not be the only decision-makers on technology acquisition.	We need to educate all stakeholders on the importance of the technology plan and provide options for everyone to comprehend how the plan will improve student learning. Also, a technology plan should highlight the aspects of the plan that will prepare students for success in the future. • Highlight patterns, critical features, big ideas, and relationships • Maximize generalization and transfer
Investment in a technology needs critical examination.	Once a draft of the technology plan is completed, all stakeholders should have an opportunity to vet critically examine the plan, and have an opportunity to provide feedback about the plan. The team should then consider, reflect on, and respond to feedback in a productive way. • Increase mastery-oriented feedback • Develop self-assessment and reflection
Detailed evaluation of technology should be done.	Districts must evaluate their current technology and its impact on students to provide background on the needs of the district. • Activate or supply background knowledge • Optimize relevance, value, and authenticity

Table 5.3: Universally designing a district technology plan (adapted from Roy & Singh, 2015) (continued)

Expert Views on Strategic Technology Planning	Implications for Universally Designed Leadership in Education
Technological success depends solely on a dedicated interdisciplinary team. Political considerations do not play an effective role in selection of technology.	Teams must contain stakeholders from all groups in order to ensure that the technology plan is relevant and valuable to the community at large. Effort must be made so the adoption of new technology does not become a political issue. • Guide appropriate goal-setting • Support planning and strategy development • Facilitate managing information and resources • Optimize relevance, value, and authenticity
Work culture is a vital consideration for selection of technology. Only a technology that fulfills the requirement of the customer should be adopted.	Districts need to build a culture where stakeholders look at technology as a tool to increase student learning. The goal of all technology purchases and initiatives should be examined through the lens of its effect on students. • Heighten salience of goals and objectives • Foster collaboration and community • Promote expectations and beliefs that optimize motivation
Feasibility study is an important factor.	The district must consider the practicality of implementing the technology plan, which is why it must align to the district's overall strategy. It must ensure that PD, capital planning, and other initiatives are in alignment. • Heighten salience of goals and objectives • Foster collaboration and community • Promote expectations and beliefs that optimize motivation

Now that you have a strong foundation, it's time to complete final preparations to build your house. Thus far, the work has been strenuous—digging deep into multiple sources of knowledge, laying down scaffolds to ensure that the base of improvements efforts is strong, and ensuring that multiple stakeholders have the opportunity to test the foundation for strength. The foundation is nearly built, but as you know, we still don't have a house. There is nowhere to return after a hard day of work to rest our feet. Really, the work has just begun.

6 Professional Development That Models UDL Principles

This chapter will address the Prepare phase with a focus on professional development. We will introduce the concept of universally designed professional development that provides options for multiple means of engagement, representation, and expression. We will offer examples of how survey data can be used to drive professional development planning that offers choices, to ensure offerings are relevant and specific to all educators regardless of grade or content area. Additionally, we will share a model of PD that fosters collaboration and community among educators and administrators.

Helmut Jahn, a world-famous German-American architect, once said, "Every building is a prototype. No two are alike." The same is true for the districts that we build. Although there are best-in-class districts that we aspire to be, the variability of our staff is too great to build a prototype. Our buildings, our staff, and our communities all exist somewhere on an infinite scale of variability. To know what is best for our district is to know our people, to collaborate with them, and to grow with them. This important work often begins and ends with the professional development we provide for our teams.

Let's don our hard hats again to return to our construction process. As we noted at the beginning of the book, every building needs a strong foundation. As a school or district leader, you must build an outstanding, well-founded system that is capable of supporting all learners and engaging them as they excel. This takes planning, collaboration, and multiple means of representation, expression, and engagement. Every tool you need in your toolbox can be found in the UDL framework.

First, you needed to explore the site and determine the needs of the land. The UDL Guidelines reminded you to recruit the interest of multiple stakeholders to develop self-assessment and reflection. This needs assessment helped you to guide appropriate goal-setting about what work needed to be completed in order to lay the foundation. Once the goal-setting process was in place, you needed to bring together the construction team to determine any problems or barriers that may affect the building process. This crucial process allowed you to minimize threats and distractions that had the potential to derail your project. Once the site work is completed and the foundation is laid, it is time to develop a strategy and provide graduated levels of support for your colleagues so everyone understands how to implement UDL to increase the outcomes of all students.

Universally designed professional development is critical in order to implement UDL as a district-wide framework. A district's most important resources are its human capital—the staff members who work to support students. Investing in these professionals ensures that all members of the teaching and learning team have a shared understanding of best practices, a commitment to the district strategy, and the ability to implement the evidence-based strategies that will result in the most effective student outcomes.

From a UDL perspective, a top-down approach to PD will not be effective. If we want our staff to become motivated, knowledgeable, strategic practitioners, we must design PD in alignment with the Guidelines. This means that in addition to multiple offerings, each individual session needs to provide options for engagement, representation, and action and expression. Each session cannot be a prototype, because prototypes simply will not allow all learners to access knowledge. A prototype can act as a scaffold as we build our own building, but it is not the building.

In order to build engagement, it's important to understand what PD is relevant and meaningful for your staff. With new initiatives required by the state, it's tempting to use available PD time to provide training on these issues of compliance or to offer PD with a prototype model, as mentioned previously. The danger of this, however, is that if teachers do not feel as though the PD is relevant, learning will not occur, and compliance will be much more difficult to achieve.

Before designing and delivering PD to staff, it's important to start with the district strategy. Since the strategy was collectively designed with all stakeholders, built on a shared vision, meaningful goals, revised with mastery-oriented feedback, and aligned to capital and technology plans, it's imperative that it is the basis for professional development so teachers can all be engaged in improving the outcomes for all students.

Collaborating with staff to define a PD calendar and PD initiatives goes a long way to increasing this engagement. Our professional development choice offerings have been a great success because they are based on evidence, involved multiple stakeholders, and celebrated and elevated our teachers to increase engagement.

The following list shows our protocol, which aims to highlight the critical features of our process. Our PD committee was instrumental in developing and implementing this protocol. You may find it helpful to use the protocol or tailor it for your own staff. (After the table, we provide a more detailed narrative of the process.)

STEPS FOR DESIGNING A HIGH-QUALITY PD SYSTEM USING UDL

1. Review relevant data on PD satisfaction and effectiveness to define areas of need.

2. Develop a collaborative professional development committee, composed of teachers and administrators.

3. Review the district strategy.

4. Complete research on PD best practices in your areas of focus.

5. Survey staff to determine PD needs to provide options for recruiting interest.

6. Put out a request for proposal (RFP) to encourage teacher leaders and administrators to develop a PD series that would align with critical areas.

7. Select courses, design a PD catalog, and have all staff members register for a course that meets their needs.

8. Provide PD-to-PD facilitators to ensure all offerings will provide multiple means of engagement, representation, and action and expression.

9. Implement multipart series, evaluating each session to encourage self-assessment and reflection.

10. Administer a final evaluation when the multipart series is complete to measure growth and gather critical need areas for the following academic year.

As we were new to this district, our work initially began with an analysis of previous PD survey results. When we looked at the data, we found that the vast majority of our teachers were not satisfied with our professional development model. It may be helpful to create a survey tool to gather baseline data from your staff so you understand the unique needs of your district. Because our baseline satisfaction results were low in indicators such as differentiation of district offerings, it allowed for us, as leaders, to comprehend the severity of need in this area. We knew that if we were going to make improvements, we would need to build collaboration and community with our teachers and professional staff. To guide this work, we developed a PD committee. This committee consisted of eight teachers and two administrators. The teachers received release time three times a year to complete this work.

Based on our analysis of the survey data, our PD committee determined our greatest needs were additional resources and time for PD, and more differentiated offerings. Every district will likely have different focus areas based on this analysis. Once we knew the area where we wanted to focus, we started researching best practices in PD related to those focus areas, since UDL is based on evidence and we needed this background knowledge in order to guide appropriate goal-setting. At this time, we had not yet developed a district strategy, so we reviewed our district improvement plan to ensure that we designed and delivered a PD program that aligned to district, school, and educator goals.

Peer-reviewed research argues that the three most important aspects in a professional development program are time span, coherence, and focus on content (Hill, 2012). Research suggests that in order to have any impact on student achievement, staff must receive a minimum of 14 hours of study in the same professional development focus area (Hill, 2012). Teachers who receive an average of 49 hours a year of substantial professional development (intensive, sustained, and strongly implemented) can boost their students' achievement by about 21 percentile points (Wei, Darling-Hammond, & Adamson, 2010).

Coherence is another important aspect of professional development, because it requires teachers to learn new content or skills, implement the new techniques, and then follow up with reflection in a future professional development session. This line of research fits in the UDL framework, since PD needs to provide options for action, expression, and reflection. Teachers cannot simply gather information. They must implement it, and reflect on its impact on their practice.

Our goal became to offer differentiated PD options, focused on content, that provided intensive, year-long study in order to be cohesive. The barrier, of course, was we didn't have a model that allowed us to offer these sessions and meet the needs of a variety of teachers. Clearly, the same offering would not meet the needs of kindergarten teachers, seventh-grade science teachers, and high-school physical education teachers. More importantly, we did not have adequate time to offer 14 hours in one content area, let alone 49. After examining our calendar, we decided to use three of the district PD half-days to offer mini-courses that would be 10 hours—much better than the previous model, which had different PD focus areas on all three days. From this, a multipart series was born.

Our multipart series turned our PD model into a system with embedded choice. Our first step was to survey teachers to ask what content or skills they needed in order to improve student outcomes. Once we had a list of critical areas, our PD committee posted a request for proposals (RFP), which outlined our need for teacher leaders and administrators to develop a PD series that would meet the needs of all our teachers. We offered stipends to any PD series that was selected, as well as supports on how to universally design the series, heighten the salience of goals, and foster collaboration and reflection throughout the series. In total, we had more than 20 multipart offerings that we compiled into a PD catalog to share with our staff. Just like in universities, our staff browsed course offerings, registered for the course of their choosing, and were contacted by the facilitator with a course outline and goals and objectives.

Because our multipart series was so successful, we partnered with a local university to encourage our staff to propose graduate courses, which would be endorsed by the university for three graduate credits. The university approves the course outlines and syllabi, as well as the instructors. This allows us to further elevate our talented staff and provides teachers with 67.5 hours of PD in the same focus area. Our first two courses? *Introduction to Universal Design for Learning* and *Mastering the Art of Writing Using Universal Design for Learning.*

We were able to make gains in our PD model by implementing cohesive, differentiated offerings, but there is always room for growth. In order to continue to increase satisfaction rates, we must eliminate some of the barriers that prevent us from offering additional resources and time for PD. We will continue to survey our staff, collect mastery-oriented feedback, and ensure that our PD focuses on improved teacher practice and student learning.

Once you have differentiated PD offerings, it's important to provide staff with resources that will allow them to design their own sessions that provide options for engagement, representation, and action and expression. As defined in the logic model in Chapter 3, "Analyzing and Interpreting the Data for the Needs Assessment," you can develop a district UDL task force who plan for future UDL full-district implementation and can be a group of educators to offer support to others, such as running a book club on the topic or teaching a multipart series on UDL.

To provide further support, we have examined each Guideline and explored what it means specifically in the design and delivery of professional development (Table 6.1).

Table 6.1: Applying the UDL Guidelines to professional development

UDL Principles →	Implement Guidelines →	What This Means for Professional Development (PD)
Provide multiple means of representation	• Provide options for perception • Offer ways of customizing the display of information • Offer alternatives for auditory information • Offer alternatives for visual information	Don't present new initiatives, research on best practices, and so on in only one way. Provide options so teachers can choose to, for example, attend a plenary session, read about the proposed initiatives, or listen to a podcast. Often PD sessions take place in large auditoriums with someone on stage "standing and delivering." Keep in mind that presentations like this are barriers to many learners.
	• Provide options for language, mathematical expressions, and symbols • Clarify vocabulary and symbols • Clarify syntax and structure • Support decoding of text, mathematical notation, and symbols • Promote understanding across languages • Illustrate through multiple media	Our staff has as much variability as our students. When preparing PD sessions, think about any specific terms that may not be familiar. Consider providing a hard copy or a link to a glossary of terms for new initiatives. Also, provide visual representations of topics under study. Instead of just presenting about UDL, for example, provide a visual representation of the three brain networks (also shown as Figure 6.1, on page 77). This is an example of illustrating through multiple media.

Table 6.1: Applying the UDL Guidelines to professional development (continued)

UDL Principles →	Implement Guidelines →	What This Means for Professional Development (PD)
	• Provide options for comprehension • Activate or supply background knowledge • Highlight patterns, critical features, big ideas, and relationships • Guide information-processing, visualization, and manipulation • Maximize transfer and generalization	When providing PD on UDL, or universally designing PD in content areas, it's crucial to show how the new initiative fits in with what teachers and staff are already doing. Time is limited, and our staff can't simply start over every time we learn more about best practices. Guide this work by making connections to other effective practices. This will activate their background knowledge and allow them to transfer new skills to their practice without throwing everything away and starting from scratch.
Provide multiple means of action and expression	• Provide options for physical action • Vary the methods for response and navigation • Optimize access to tools and assistive technologies	During PD sessions, provide opportunities for learners to get up and collaborate in person, interact with online modules, or use multimedia tools or assistive technology to express what they are learning to reinforce how to implement new skills with students. Even short movement breaks can increase engagement and activate the brain.
	• Provide options for expression and communication • Use multiple media for communication • Use multiple tools for construction and composition • Build fluencies with graduated levels of support for practice and performance	As research suggested, teachers need to apply new content they learn in PD and reflect on the implementation process. Providing options for teachers to implement and share this work is invaluable. For example, teachers can be encouraged to design lessons and then write a reflection on how the lesson went, or bring in student work that resulted from the lesson. Providing exemplars, templates, and rubrics allows learners to access support that will guide them as they implement new knowledge and skills with their students.

Table 6.1: Applying the UDL Guidelines to professional development (continued)

UDL Principles →	Implement Guidelines →	What This Means for Professional Development (PD)
	• Provide options for executive functions • Guide appropriate goal-setting • Support planning and strategy development • Facilitate managing information and resources • Enhance capacity for monitoring progress	Having clear goals for PD sessions is only the first step of building executive function. It's also important to ask learners to set their own goals for the PD session or series. They may want to create a strategy, or a to-do list, of how they will implement the information gathered in PD. Also, make it clear what participants will be able to do as a result of the PD session. This will allow them to monitor their progress throughout the session.
Provide multiple means of engagement	• Provide options for recruiting interest • Optimize individual choice and autonomy • Optimize relevance, value, and authenticity • Minimize threats and distractions	You need to attract people's attention before you can teach them anything or share information with them. This is why it is important to share how the work will be meaningful by connecting it to the needs of the district. If this is done well, you won't have anyone in a PD session that says, "Why are we learning this anyway?"
	• Provide options for sustaining effort and persistence • Heighten salience of goals and objectives • Vary demands and resources to optimize challenge • Foster collaboration and community • Increase mastery-oriented feedback	Recruiting interest is simple. Maintaining interest is the work. This is why it is important to offer opportunities for collaboration and discuss the importance of a growth mindset. Some learners may feel overwhelmed by new initiatives, may fear the unknown, or may feel as though what they are doing is more effective. This is why it's important to remind attendees of the research underlying each session and the goals of the session. Also, anticipate the challenges so you have coping strategies in place.

Table 6.1: Applying the UDL Guidelines to professional development (continued)

UDL Principles →	Implement Guidelines →	What This Means for Professional Development (PD)
	• Provide options for self-regulation • Promote expectations and beliefs that optimize motivation • Facilitate personal coping skills and strategies • Develop self-assessment and reflection	Lastly, we must develop self-assessment and reflection in our PD facilitators and our teachers. This allows everyone to reflect on their learning and it also improves future PD offerings. Collecting feedback throughout and at the completion of the session ensures that the session or the attendees don't go too far off track.

Figure 6.1: Three learning networks © 2013 CAST, Inc. Used with permission.

To build capacity in your district, make sure your staff members are given adequate support to improve their practice, and universally design and deliver learning experiences that meet the needs of all students, in alignment with your district strategy and vision. The most effective way to do this is to model the strategies that result in the most positive outcomes. Collaborating with a PD committee to ensure differentiated offerings, and providing support to PD facilitators are important steps in building the foundation of a successful, best-in-class district.

As you have learned, it is critical to integrate all aspects of the organization as you explore UDL and prepare to implement UDL as a district-wide framework. At this point, we'd like to offer a visual representation (Table 6.2) of the connection between the important phases we've discussed in the text and how they are all critical components when building the foundation for success for all learners.

Table 6.2: Explore and prepare in preparation to build

Explore	Prepare
• Examine multiple sources of knowledge to understand UDL, district culture, strengths, and needs. • Build a culture of evidence-based decision-making and mastery-oriented feedback. • Complete a comprehensive needs assessment to identify specific problem statements. • Build a logic model to drive the district strategy.	• Create a shared vision with all stakeholders to lay the groundwork for the construction of a strategy that will support UDL implementation. • Use the needs assessment and the logic model to build a district strategy that includes specific actionable steps and facilitates the management of information and resources. • Encourage educators to build their goals around district and school goals that speak to the need for UDL implementation. • Provide professional development to support future implementation of UDL, district-wide.

7

UDL in the Classroom

This chapter will introduce the Integration phase through the lens of supporting implementation and evaluating effectiveness during teacher observation and evaluation. The chapter will discuss resources that will help educators align their practice to UDL expectations in order to improve their performance on their district evaluation tool. We will also provide sample UDL-aligned educator evaluation resources.

The data has been analyzed, the district strategy is designed, and professional development has been implemented. Now it's time to monitor your progress, and that takes the form of observing UDL implementation in action.

Observing a universally designed classroom can feel intimidating if the evaluator has not been extensively trained in UDL pedagogy. This is often the case. While we recommend evaluators be trained in UDL, it is not necessary for purposes of observation. What is necessary is an understanding of what UDL is and what good UDL instruction looks like. Just as planning for UDL implementation at the district level takes time and commitment, so, too, does planning for classroom implementation.

Observing Teachers

One fact that you may not know is that many students in college preparation programs are now being trained in UDL practices. The 2008 Higher Education Opportunity Act (Public Law 110-315) requires recipients of Teacher Quality Partnership Grants and Teach to Reach Grants to offer preparation programs that enable teachers to understand and use "strategies consistent with the principles of Universal Design for Learning" and "to integrate technology effectively into curricula and instruction, including technology consistent with the principles of Universal Design for Learning." In addition, the HEOA encourages colleges and universities to incorporate UDL into evaluation and performance measures for their teacher-education programs. Many top-tier colleges and universities offer courses or extensive course content in Universal Design for Learning.

A resource derived from work done at the East Carolina University with students in a rural, special-education teacher preparation program may provide insight into how colleges and universities are integrating UDL into their preparation programs. Evans, Williams, King, and Metcalf (2010) describe the way East Carolina embeds UDL expectations into its preparation program in the areas of assessment, classroom management, and planning.

One way to support UDL practices in newly hired staff is to integrate UDL principles into the staff induction program in your school or district. You can also embed it into the training modules of the mentor program or during mentor training. You can also easily integrate components of UDL into the observation forms that mentors use. This, of course, requires you to provide training on UDL to the district mentor coordinator and all trained mentors. A district may even want to consider making UDL training or experience a requirement of the induction program.

Veteran staff can also be observed through the UDL lens. In order to support this work, it's important to make explicit connections between the district's current evaluation tool and the UDL framework. Many districts across the country use educator evaluation systems that focus on similar domains. Often, these domains are based on the Framework for Teaching (The Danielson Group, 2013). The Framework for Teaching is a research-based set of components of instruction, focused on four domains: planning and preparation, classroom environment, instruction, and professional responsibilities. In the Massachusetts Model System for Educator Evaluation, there are four domains, or standards, for educators including curriculum instruction and assessment, teaching all students, family and community engagement, and professional responsibility. A closer examination of the elements beneath each standard reflects how closely the expected responsibilities of teachers align to the UDL framework.

Table 7.1 presents specific language from the Massachusetts Model System for Educator Evaluation teacher rubric (Massachusetts Department Education, 2015) that examines that state's standard of "teaching all students" and alludes directly to UDL. You can create a similar crosswalk by comparing the UDL Guidelines to the language in your rubric.

Table 7.1: Examining the educator rubric for "Teaching All Students" through a UDL lens

Teaching All Students	Specific Rubric Language	Alignment with UDL Guidelines
Instruction	"Consistently defines high expectations for the quality of student work and the perseverance and effort required to produce it; often provides exemplars, rubrics, and guided practice" "Likely to motivate and engage most students during the lesson" "Uses appropriate practices, including tiered instruction and scaffolds"	• Provide options for sustaining effort and persistence • Build fluencies with graduated levels of support for practice and performance • Provide options for recruiting interest • Promote expectations and beliefs that optimize motivation
Learning environment	"Provides opportunities for students to learn in groups with diverse peers" "Consistently creates learning experiences that guide students to identify their strengths, interests, and needs"	• Foster collaboration and community • Enhance capacity for monitoring progress • Develop self-assessment and reflection
Cultural proficiency	"Actively creates and maintains an environment in which students' diverse backgrounds, identities, strengths, and challenges are respected"	• Optimize relevance, value, and authenticity • Minimize threats and distractions
Expectations	"Effectively models and reinforces ways that students can master challenging material through effective effort, rather than having to depend on innate ability"	• Provide options for sustaining effort and persistence • Promote expectations and beliefs that optimize motivation

Once you have created an alignment between your own educator evaluation tool and UDL, share the results with your educators to make explicit connections among the district strategy and district goals, and their own

SMART goals, educator evaluation, and UDL so they realize that the frame-work supports all district functions. This will increase engagement in UDL, as the framework provides them with specific strategies to increase student outcomes and improve their own performance.

When administrators have a shared understanding of the alignment between the educator rubrics and UDL, they can help to support the integration of strategies that will improve their instructional leadership.

UDL Rubrics

If you are in a district where you have the opportunity to collectively bargain your own educator evaluation system rubric, you can align the rubrics to UDL to support the Integration phase. The Bartholomew Consolidated School Corporation (BCSC) has incorporated UDL practices as the single biggest percentage of their educator evaluation framework (50 percent). Earlier, we discussed ways to support leaders in their work on UDL such as an adminis-tration-only UDL course. BCSC does this explicitly by incorporating UDL into all of the educator rubrics (including for administrators). Figures 7.1–7.3 show the rubrics that are used in BCSC's process. These evaluation rubrics represent expectations for UDL for teachers, as well as leaders (see the Appendix on page 105 for full-size rubrics).

Figure 7.1: Sample BCSC evaluation rubrics

BCSC
2014-15 DEAN/COUNSELOR SUCCESS RUBRIC

DEAN/COUNSELOR BEING EVALUATED

EVALUATOR

		INEFFECTIVE (1)	NEEDS IMPROVEMENT (2)	EFFECTIVE (3)	HIGHLY EFFECTIVE (4)
INSTRUCTIONAL FRAMEWORK	UDL	€ School wide goals are not known	€ School wide goals are known but not addressed or instructional resources are not aligned with the goals	€ School wide goals are known and instructional resources align with the goal	€ School wide goals are known, attainable and accessible. Instructional resources align with the goal
		€ Potential barriers are not considered during the planning of the interaction or the design of the learning environment	€ Potential barriers are considered but the building administrator is not applying that knowledge to the interaction	€ Potential barriers are considered and the building administrator applies that knowledge to the learning environment	€ Potential barriers related to the resources, information, and learning environment are identified and addressed in the design of the interaction and the learning environment
		€ Content and skills are presented without options and scaffolding	€ Content is presented with few options and skills are presented without scaffolding	€ Content and skills are presented in multiple ways with options but with minimal scaffolding	€ Content and skills are presented in multiple ways with options and scaffolding available
		€ The students and/or parents are not engaged	€ The students and/or parents are engaged in relevant learning opportunities	€ The students and/or parents are engaged in relevant and meaningful learning opportunities	€ The students and/or parents are engaged in authentic, relevant, and meaningful learning opportunities
		€ The students do not demonstrate and articulate appropriate choices	€ The students rarely demonstrate and articulate appropriate choices	€ The students occasionally demonstrate and articulate appropriate choices	€ The students consistently demonstrate and articulate appropriate choices

Figure 7.2: Sample BCSC evaluation rubrics (continued)

BCSC
2014-15 BUILDING ADMINISTRATOR SUCCESS RUBRIC

ADMINISTRATOR BEING EVALUATED

EVALUATOR

		INEFFECTIVE (1)	NEEDS IMPROVEMENT (2)	EFFECTIVE (3)	HIGHLY EFFECTIVE (4)
INSTRUCTIONAL FRAMEWORK	UDL	€ School wide goals are not known	€ School wide goals are known but not addressed or instructional resources are not aligned with the goals	€ School wide goals are known and instructional resources align with the goal	€ School wide goals are known, attainable, and accessible. Instructional resources align with the goal
		€ Potential barriers are not considered during the planning of the interaction or the design of the learning environment	€ Potential barriers are considered but the building administrator is not applying that knowledge to the interaction	€ Potential barriers are considered and the building administrator applies that knowledge to the learning environment	€ Potential barriers related to the resources, information and learning environment are identified and addressed in the design of the interaction and the learning environment
		€ Content and skills are presented without options and scaffolding	€ Content is presented with few options and skills are presented without scaffolding	€ Content and skills are presented in multiple ways with options but with minimal scaffolding	€ Content and skills are presented in multiple ways with options and scaffolding available
		€ The school community members are not engaged	€ The school community members are engaged in relevant learning opportunities	€ The school community members are engaged in relevant and meaningful learning opportunities	€ The school community members are engaged in authentic, relevant and meaningful learning opportunities
		€ The school community members do not interact with or demonstrate content and skill comprehension	€ The school community members interact with content and skill comprehension but do not demonstrate knowledge	€ The school community members interact with and demonstrate content and skill comprehension in multiple ways	€ The school community members consistently interact with and demonstrate content and skill comprehension in multiple ways

Figure 7.3: Sample BCSC evaluation rubrics (continued)

Statewide Support

As we mentioned previously, No Child Left Behind (NCLB) was replaced with the Every Student Succeeds Act (ESSA) of 2015, where UDL is defined and endorsed. In addition to efforts at the federal level, some state departments of education have required Universal Design for Learning. For example, Maryland's 2010 UDL bill (HB 59/SB 467) led to the creation of a statewide task force.

While not all states have specific laws, more and more state departments of education are creating and sharing UDL-based resources. For example, understanding the need to integrate multiple areas of important work occurring in any one district, the Massachusetts Department of Elementary and Secondary Education developed the *Educator Effectiveness Guidebook for Inclusive Practice* (2015a) to supplement their new educator evaluation system. This guidebook describes its purpose: "Working with educational researchers and Massachusetts educators, designers wove strategies for best instructional practice and behavioral support throughout the Guidebook to provide a common language and consistent set of expectations. The tools of the Guidebook align to evidence-based best practice by following the principles of Universal Design for Learning (UDL) . . ." (p 2).

The guidebook provides sample educator goals that articulate UDL principles, speaking directly to the use of multiple means of representation, engagement, and action and expression. Figures 7.4–7.5 show how the department aligns UDL principles, framed in a case study, with professional practice and student learning goals.

As showcased in the logic model for UDL implementation, UDL training must not be exclusive to teachers. Administrators must also have a firm handle on what good universally designed practice looks like. In addition, focusing on aspects of the educator evaluation framework that relate to Universal Design for Learning allows evaluators the support and tools to provide meaningful feedback to staff. Providing tools such as exemplar UDL-based goals, offering sample universally designed artifacts of practice, and showcasing examples of what observers should be looking for in UDL classrooms allow for more consistent practices as they relate to UDL and educator evaluation.

CASE STUDY EDUCATOR 1:
Sixth-Grade Science Teacher Targeting Multiple Means of Representation

Mr. Thompson has a sixth-grade science class of 25 students, including eight students with learning disabilities, one student on the autism spectrum, and two students in the gifted and talented range. Previous evaluators have noted Mr. Thompson's reliance on teacher-directed instruction in which students listen to a lecture, take notes, and are invited to ask questions as needed. Demonstration of student understanding tends to be through short essay responses on worksheets and assessments. Although no attendance or behavior issues were observed, not all students in the class consistently complete the work that is assigned, and many struggle on the differentiated cumulative end-of-unit assessments. For example, only 12 of Mr. Thompson's students earned a passing score of at least 75 percent on the differentiated Unit 1 end-of-unit assessment.

Professional Practice Goal

By April 2016, Mr. Thompson will incorporate at least one alternative method of representation of course content, appropriate for the individual needs within his classroom, into 100 percent of the lessons he teaches as measured by observation feedback, planning documentation, and student work samples.

Student Learning Goal

In order to improve student performance in his sixth-grade earth science class, Mr. Thompson will incorporate multiple means of representation of course content so that all students earn a passing score of at least 75 percent on the differentiated cumulative end-of-unit assessment by April 2016.

Figure 7.4: Department's alignment of UDL principles

CASE STUDY EDUCATOR 3:
Fifth-Grade General Education and Special Education Mathematics Co-Teachers Targeting Multiple Means of Action and Expression

A general education teacher and a special education teacher co-teach a fifth-grade inclusion class. There are 24 students in the class, and eight students have IEPs (individualized education programs). The teachers work together for the duration of the school day and share a common planning period. The two teachers have agreed on a collaborative student learning goal that will measure mathematics growth. The results of the beginning-of-year mathematics assessment show 67 percent of students in the class achieved a score of at least 50 percent, and 33 percent of the class scored below 50 percent on the beginning-of-year mathematics assessment.

This is the first year that these teachers have co-taught together, and they have found that they have varying styles of assessing student learning. The general education teacher prefers to assess formative learning through written exit tickets at the end of every class. Some students struggle to complete the exit ticket in the allotted time. The special education teacher likes to assess formative learning through frequent verbal checks for understanding throughout the lesson. Some students respond well to this method, but other students who tend to be quieter are easily overlooked and are struggling with the content. Summative assessments in the class are almost exclusively pencil-and-paper tests and quizzes. The school has access to document cameras, iPads, interactive whiteboards, and student polling devices, but these tools are not currently used in the classroom.

Professional Practice Goal

By April 2016, the co-teachers will include at least two alternative media for students to communicate their learning into 100 percent of the lessons that the educators teach as measured by samples of student work and observation feedback.

Student Learning Goal

In order to improve mastery of fifth-grade mathematics skills, the co-teachers will allow students to communicate their learning through assessments using multiple media so that 100 percent of students will demonstrate moderate to high growth in mathematics as evidenced by performance on beginning- and end-of-year assessments.

Figure 7.5: Department's alignment of UDL principles

Source: Massachusetts Department of Education Evaluation http://www.doe.mass.edu/edeval/guidebook/Guidebook.pdf

8

UDL and the Art of the Meeting

This chapter will continue the Integrate phase by showcasing how to apply UDL to instructional practices and decision-making. The intent of this work is to model the practices of universally designed leadership and to ensure the engagement of the leadership team around the benefits of UDL implementation. By immersing your educators and administrators in universally designed meetings, you can allow them to experience the principles of UDL in practice. This is accomplished by providing concrete examples of how to universally design and deliver meetings.

Thomas Sowell, a senior fellow at Stanford University, said the following about meetings: "People who enjoy meetings should not be in charge of anything." When we consider how most meetings are run, we may find some truth in this statement. I am sure you can recall many meetings you have attended that were a colossal waste of time. However, leaders can increase engagement and productivity at meetings, if they are designed and delivered using the UDL Guidelines. We even argue that meetings can be fun.

Of course, it's deflating to attend a PD session or planning meeting on UDL that is not universally designed. Participants feel the contradiction right away. Sure, developing a meeting using the UDL framework takes time. But it's worth it. Give yourself and your team the time you need to plan meetings, PD sessions, and related materials in a universally designed manner. Keep the UDL Guidelines on hand as you plan. Use them as a checklist to ensure that you are meeting those expectations in your planning and delivery.

In our district, we created a UDL task force to help to guide the integration of UDL in all learning environments. For our first meeting, it was important for us to universally design the agenda so we could begin to model how the UDL framework can increase engagement and learning outcomes. With the UDL task force co-chair, a seventh-grade math teacher, we developed an agenda that incorporates the UDL principles.

The agenda in Table 8.1 is intentional in its universal design. The meeting materials themselves took into consideration multiple means of engagement by recruiting interest, sustaining effort throughout various activities, and defining opportunities for self-regulation. It is specific about representing material, with attention to perception, language, and comprehension. It also offers multiple means of action and expression in the various approaches to communication, as well as the planning around executive function. When we shared the agenda, we did so in Google Drive so all committee members could customize the display of information, build background knowledge of meeting expectations, and guide appropriate goal-setting.

Table 8.1: Sample agenda for universally designed meeting

Agenda for UDL Task Force

Resources and information that will be provided at the meeting:
- Color copies of MTSS model
- Color copies of UDL Guidelines
- Copies of MTSS data (barriers)

Introductions and icebreaker: Show and tell to build collaboration and community.

Please bring one or more items, photos, special possessions, or similar to share with the group. You have two minutes to introduce yourself and share who you are and why your show-and-tell item will help us to get to know you a bit better. (It can be personal or professional! Your choice!)

Engagement: Why are we doing this work? (Full group)
- Explain MTSS model breakout and map current MTSS resources that are available to all students by school (compare to MTSS model)
- Twenty-first century skills and explicit connection to UDL (jigsaw)
- Review MTSS data: What barriers will we face? (jigsaw)
- How do we integrate the growth mindset work?

Representation: What work are we doing? (Full group)
- What is MTSS? (Options for representation—quick presentation)
- What is UDL? (Options for representation—quick presentation; focus group to reflect on implementation from summer course)

Table 8.1: Sample agenda for universally designed meeting (continued)

Agenda for UDL Task Force

Action and Expression: How will we do this work? (Small group)

Executive function group:

- What's our goal for this year? What can we actually accomplish this year? Is it different by Tier?
- What does that look like?
- What is our five-year plan?

Collaboration group:

- How do we get everyone's voices so our decisions and plan reflect all stakeholder voices?
- How will we collaborate with the co-chairs of the teacher induction program, education evaluation working group (inclusive practice), and professional development committee to ensure all district groups are committed to our plan? (e.g., How do we train all district staff in UDL? Do we need a "train the trainer" time?)
- How can we create structures for parents to be more involved in this process?

Schedule the next meeting and create an agenda.

Homework:

Optional links to review/refresh on UDL

Universally designing a meeting agenda represents one area of leadership to model. We suggest this level of planning be completed for all meeting materials. Table 8.2 shows a portion of a map provided to our colleagues that illustrates two key focus areas for our leadership team's work during a summer administrative retreat. It was a supplement to our retreat agenda. It aligns the standards we are evaluated under, articulates necessary schema, and highlights the portions of the agenda that relate to this key focus area. The overt and bolded references to the UDL Guidelines are there in order to model the alignment of UDL in our work.

The agenda and meeting materials are only as good as the activities that we engage in during our meetings. Table 8.2 is an example of a map provided to our colleagues that illustrates the two key focus areas for our leadership team's work. One of the agenda topics, *"Challenge 1: Vision for Information Use"* is annotated in Table 8.3 to highlight some of the Guidelines that are incorporated in this one challenge. This is just one universally designed activity. (We will provide additional activities and resources in the forthcoming companion guidebook, *Resources for Implementing Universally Designed Leadership.*)

Table 8.2: Sample meeting resource to highlight patterns and critical features of UDL

Information -Based Decision-Making:	MTSS and UDL PD:
Evaluation standards adjustment to practice: Provides planning time and effective support for teams to review assessment data **(Provide options for executive functions)** and identify appropriate interventions and adjustments to practice **(Provide options for self-regulation)**. Monitors educators' efforts and successes in this area (MA DESE, 2012).	**Evaluation standards** Leads all educators and teams to reflect on the effectiveness of lessons, units, and interactions with students **(Provide options for self-regulation)**. Ensures that staff use data, research, and best practices to adapt instruction to achieve improved results (MA DESE, 2012).

Necessary background information **(Provide options for comprehension)**

- A cohesive vision for information use in the district to heighten the goal of data work **(Provide options for sustaining effort and persistence)**
- A firm understanding of where the district is on the spectrum of information-based decision-making
- Practical experience with setting up conditions for collaborative team inquiry **(Provide options for sustaining effort and persistence)**
- Exposure to and use of instructional data meeting protocols to support understanding of our data-analysis strategy **(Provide options for executive functions)**
- Understanding and use of multiple data sets **(Provide options for expression and communication)**

Necessary background information: **(Provide options for comprehension)**

- How do MTSS and UDL relate to the district's problem statements?
- The research base around the effectiveness of MTSS and UDL
- An understanding of all UDL Guidelines and how they translate into meaningful learning experiences for all learners

Related retreat agenda topics:

- Challenge 1: Vision for Information Use
- Data Race
- Data Vision Drafting
- Using Information Wisely
- Reviewing the Success and Distress of Past Program Cuts and Initiatives

Related retreat agenda topics:

- Universal Design for Learning 101
- Universal Design for Learning 102
- Multi-Tiered System of Support: UDL
- Using Information Wisely: UDL
- Introduction to Observing UDL Practices in the Classroom

Table 8.3: Universally designed vision activity for administrative retreat

Beginning to Develop a Vision for Information Based Decision-Making (1 Hour, 45 Minutes)

Purpose

- UDL Highlight—Principle III. Provide Multiple Means of Engagement. Focus on providing options for recruiting interest and options that foster collaboration and community.
- Model the development of a cohesive vision for data/information use in the district.
- Provide practical experience with setting up conditions for collaborative team inquiry.

Alignment to Administrative State Evaluation Standards

- Adjustment to Practice: Provides planning time and effective support for teams to review assessment data and identify appropriate interventions and adjustments to practice. Monitors educators' efforts and successes in this area (MA DESE, 2012).

Goals/Objectives

- Successfully use communication skills to manage the physical challenge as a group. Produce a draft vision statement for your group.
- Highlight UDL Principle I. Provide Multiple Means of Representation: Activate or supply background knowledge by reviewing Background/Prior Knowledge Schema (Links to Documents and Presentation were provided electronically along with print versions.)

Assessment

Each member of the retreat will use a private ballot to vote for the winning team. They will decide based on the content of the vision statement. They are not allowed to vote for their own team. The winner of the challenge will be provided a token.

Instructional Methods

First, get into your designated teams. Each team will be given one soft/squishy ball and one slingshot. One member will use their bandana as a blindfold and be placed on a taped mark (Mark A). One other member is going to be placed on Mark B, blindfolded as well. It is up to the other three members to only use words (no physical contact) to coach their colleague with the slingshot to successfully shoot the ball into the bowl that team member two is holding. One of these three members will also be expected to pick up the ball and get it back into the slingshot if it misses the mark [provide options for physical action]. Upon completion of the physical task, your team can move onto the vision development protocol (see below).

Developing a Vision Statement Protocol (Adapted from Geier & Smith, 2012)

Writing a succinct, meaningful, vision statement by committee is virtually impossible. It is, however, not only possible, but desirable to have a group provide input on the content of the statement and delegate one or two team members to draft the statement [Promote expectations and beliefs that optimize motivation]. The following steps will help each team member use the shared strategic focus to contribute to the draft vision statement.

Table 8.3: Universally designed vision activity for administrative retreat (continued)

Beginning to Develop a Vision for Information Based Decision-Making (1 Hour, 45 Minutes)

1. Choose a team facilitator. The facilitator should write the following sentence starter on a new piece of chart paper. We have provided this scaffold to help build fluencies with graduated levels of support.

> **Our district will** *"accomplish"* by *"methods or strategies"* that will be used to achieve the vision.

For Example	For Example
Use data to...	Creating school data teams
Collect and analyze data to...	Collecting and disseminating high-quality date in a timely manner
Create a culture of data use...	Supporting data use to inform all decisions
Support the use of data by all staff members.	
Inform all decisions with data.	
Allocate resources based on analysis of relevant data.	

Example of a completed statement: Our district will use data to inform all decisions by collecting and disseminating high-quality data to all stakeholders in a timely manner.

2. Each member of the team should use the sentence starter as a guide to help them write a draft vision statement.

3. Please write out your sentence on the chart paper and then represent the statement in one of the following manners. You have a number of options for action and expression:
   - A visual representation of the vision (a picture or photograph)
   - A small paragraph describing what the vision statement looks like in practice
   - A song with lyrics that depict the vision statement
   - A small skit that acts out your vision statement
   - A PowerPoint or Prezi that describes the vision statement

4. When requested to do so, share your team's statement via multiple means of expression.

5. Turn in the chart paper statements, which will be compiled during a break to be used for a later activity. These draft statements will be collectively reviewed and refined by the whole group in a later session of the retreat.

The work of planning meetings should not be reserved for the staff. Support for UDL must be inclusive of the full stakeholder group, so having all members experience universally designed meetings is a great tool to build their under-standing of its effectiveness. Table 8.4 shows an example of an activity that you could use with your school board to review a recent presentation from your UDL task force.

Table 8.4: School board choice activity

Meeting Reflection: Multiple Means of Action and Expression
Provide one example of how you have a better understanding of the work that the UDL task force has done to date by choosing one of the following options: • Express your new understanding in haiku form or in a three- to five-line poem or song (you are free to sing it when we share). • Draw a comic that represents your new understanding. • Tweet your new understanding using the district hashtag. • Write a short (one-paragraph) reflection about your new understanding. • Write a script for a short infomercial about the work of the steering committee. • Choreograph and perform an interpretative dance about your process of learning. • Roll the dice!

This chapter presents but a few examples of UDL in action. It's important to remember that when integrating UDL, the framework must be present in all aspects of district operation. The district strategy will be focused and will only note the implementation of UDL using specific action steps. As leaders, you can improve the overall integration of UDL by modeling the framework in meetings, and hopefully, you can build engagement and maybe, just maybe, have a little fun.

9 UDL Family-Community Engagement

This final chapter addresses fostering collaboration and supporting the integration of UDL as a component of the Integrate phase. The chapter will define tools to get parents and the community actively involved and supporting UDL practices and principles. We will provide some samples of how to provide multiple means of engagement, representation, and action and expression, including options such as integrating UDL strategy into school news and press releases, inviting families and communities to universally designed meetings and community information offerings, and providing multiple options for families and communities to monitor the district's progress toward meeting identified goals. The chapter will conclude with a strategy for developing two-way communication models to meet the needs of all stakeholders for the entire Integrate phase.

In an inspiring TED Talk, entrepreneur Derek Sivers (2010) shares a video that shows viewers how to start a movement in less than three minutes. The star of the video is a concert-goer, dancing alone in a field at a music festival. He was passionately dancing, and everyone else was sitting around or staring. Then, one person joined him, then another, and then hundreds danced along with him. We recently shared Sivers's TED Talk with our administrative team to demonstrate that one person alone can inspire a movement.

We asked the administrators to think about something they were passionate about, write it down or draw it, and dance about it. We encouraged this silliness to show a point. When you are a leader, you often have to be the first one out in public talking about something new. You have to be willing to be that first lone dancer, and such an action takes courage and the ability to get out of your comfort zone.

As you introduce your community to the concept of UDL, you may find yourself feeling self-conscious as you stand alone. But, UDL is infectious, and within a short amount of time, you will see your community will begin to dance behind and beside you. Why? Because it benefits students, and when something measurably benefits students, people begin to "dance."

In the architectural stages of UDL building, members of an involved school community will often describe Universal Design for Learning as "just another initiative." The single biggest factor in this statement is the misunderstanding about what UDL is. Equivalent to the concept of a diet versus a change in lifestyle, Universal Design for Learning is less a new *thing* to do and more an *approach* to the work we already do. One of the easiest ways to foster collaboration and support for UDL is to explain what it is and to show what it looks like. How do you accomplish this? Similar to how we universally design all introductions, exposure, learning, and planning of UDL with staff, we need to universally design community engagement so they experience it firsthand, along with being explicit about the benefits of UDL.

Many districts spend most of their time on public relations communication along with efforts for public participation. We send out newsletters and press releases about what is going well in our district. In regards to public participation, we invite the public to come into our schools to volunteer in our classrooms. While public relations and public participation are important, community engagement represents so much more. If we are brave, we will be clear with the community about not only what we are doing well but areas for growth. As we shared in the beginning of this book, we need to engage them in this work, so we can, as a community, build a network of support for the improvement work to come. It not only defines a sense of community, but ownership over the process. No longer are they at the will of the schools to perform well or to help with property values, but they own a piece of this responsibility, and thus become equal advocates when needs are articulated. Community engagement, according to the not-for-profit Harwood Institute for Public Innovation (as cited in Illinois Association of School Boards [IASB], 2013), involves these key principles or values:

- Ongoing public engagement, not just one-time public input
- Connecting with citizens as owners, not as customers
- Reflecting different voices or viewpoints, not just geography or demographics
- Building common ground, not just consensus
- Creating knowledge, not just providing information

Table 9.1 provides examples of how the principles of UDL support community engagement using language consistent with the UDL Guidelines 2.0.

Table 9.1: Community engagement in UDL alignment

Community Engagement Principle	UDL Principle	Explanation
Ongoing public engagement	Multiple means of engagement	In order to foster sustained attention and effort, it is essential to find relevance and saliency in this work for all stakeholders.
Citizens as owners	Multiple means of engagement	Stakeholders differ significantly in what attracts their attention and engages their interest. Thus, it is essential to understand those interests and utilize them in your work with that stakeholder group. If they relate personally and purposefully to the benefits of UDL, they take a sense of ownership over it, rather than being passive recipients of it.
Differing views and voices	Multiple means of representation	It's necessary to provide information about UDL through different modalities (hearing about it, reading about it, and so on) and to provide information in a format that will allow for adjustability by the user (e.g., text that can be enlarged for members of the audience who may be unable to read small print, sounds that can be amplified).
Building common ground	Multiple means of expression	At the highest level of the human capacity is to set long-term goals, plan effective strategies for reaching those goals, monitor their progress, and modify strategies as needed. We need to support this work with all stakeholders as we drive toward our shared vision using all available resources.
Creating knowledge	Multiple means of representation	The purpose is to teach learners how to transform accessible information into usable knowledge. How can UDL work to better the district and community?

Multiple Means of Engagement

When you work with various stakeholders, you will undoubtedly have variability in their understanding and comfort with education, your school system, and student needs. The way to address this is to provide varied demands and offer varied resources to stakeholders throughout the UDL implementation process. At the beginning of the text, we focused on the need for community engagement during the Explore phase, but it doesn't end there. Community involvement must be continuous.

For example, when working with a group of local citizens, some are recently retired teachers with a lot of background schema. Don't waste their time educating them about the realities of public education today, or the needs. They know the needs, since they lived it. With a group like this, tap into their knowledge and ask what they wished they had done to meet the needs of all learners? Ask them to articulate the frustrations of meeting the needs of all learners in a traditional educational approach. While you may have one group of previous educators in your group, others are very removed from the context of public education and may have been since they attended school. They do not have a common understanding of the current challenges that face schools today. We once heard from someone who wanted to know why we are concerned with our resources since they had 40 students in their class.

However, when those 40 students were in that class, the school did not support any special education students or English language learners; it did not have high-stakes accountability measures, nor did it have to wrangle with competing for the attention of students with mobile devices and social media. Although it may be tempting to share information about how outdated their notions of education are, this has the potential to be insulting.

Instead, provide options for breakout groups. For example, your leadership team can provide options for community members to delve into important research that will help them to understand the current realities of education in your district. When marketing these opportunities, it would be valuable to share who your intended audience is, or the level of background knowledge that is appropriate for each of the different groups, so community members can reflect on their current knowledge and select the best option. This will ensure that their participation is valuable to them.

To recruit all learners into this work in a way that they are equally invested, we must pay attention to the work in regard to relevance, value, and authenticity. We must identify the different stakeholders and define what they value, what is relevant to their lives, and what work is meaningful. In a framework of external stakeholders, Weerts and Hudson (2009) discuss the use of the organization's mission as a compass that guides stakeholder engagement. Their work is in relation to higher education, but their principles of identifying external stakeholders, such as legislators, the greater public, and alumni, and marketing to them, along with engaging with them in meaningful ways, is a template K–12 can use as well.

One way to organize and articulate this engagement with multiple stakeholders is through a stakeholder map. It defines the stakeholder group, articulates their interests in supporting this work (for example, for the greater community the benefits may be something like workforce development, educated citizenry, or high property values), and outlines the communication offered around our introduction and implementation of Universal Design for Learning. Using work by Curtis and City (2009) to articulate stakeholder interests, one can outline various stakeholder groups; articulate what is valuable, relevant, and meaningful to them; and articulate your work to engage them with those areas in mind.

For example, when working with faculty, their interests may be to ensure positive impacts on students, to know what is expected of them, to ensure that it supports their practice, to understand that the district has respect for their competence and professionalism, to ensure the union contracts are followed, and to ensure that strategy supports and respects staff.

The general public's interests may differ. They may be more interested in workforce development, educated citizenry, property values inherent with good school systems, and overall community health. We must speak about the need for UDL in respect to these interests throughout our implementation process. We must make the work relevant. If we meet the needs of all learners, how will this provide a stable workforce, how will these students engage in the community, and how will this translate to positive measures of performance and raise property values?

Multiple Means of Representation

By engaging in multiple means of representation, leaders can address the varied viewpoints of their community, build common ground, and create a foundation for common knowledge on the subject of UDL.

A good first step is to determine who your community stakeholders are, what communication methods work best for engaging them, and what information you want to give and receive. Cox (2014) notes that,"Purposeful communication is most effective when it is valuable to stakeholders." Use the knowledge gained from the assessment of stakeholders or an interest survey of those stakeholders to assess their preferred communication methods in order to create a communication strategy serviceable to each group.

For example, parents and families of students are a critical stakeholder group. For this group, one easy technique is to use captive time during open houses or similar events to conduct a communications survey, and follow up with an online survey for those who prefer this method. Find out what communication methods they prefer and what information is of most interest. For example, if majority prefer the website or e-mails, you should put your energy into sharing information about UDL by developing and sharing a new UDL webpage on the district site, creating video blogs about UDL in action and hosting them online, and creating a schedule of regular e-mails of UDL information-sharing to be pushed out to the group. This information, however, must be supplemented with mailings, presentations, and even informational phone calls if necessary.

Education about what UDL is, and how the framework lays the foundation for important district work, helps to separate it from other initiatives. It is essential to strip community-based information of educational jargon or define those elements that will not be understood by the overall public. Customize your information to them and to their interests. Give it in bite-size chunks. In one district, the parents may be very concerned about the achievement gap of certain subgroups, another may be interested in the overall implementation of new curriculum, while another may ask how UDL will meet the needs of accelerated students. Since UDL is intended to meet the needs of all learners, it is helpful to customize your communications with particular interests so the community can choose to explore the resources that are most relevant to them. In short, you have to make UDL relevant to all learners in your community so they can support the variability of all learners in the district.

When engaging in community outreach about UDL, it is helpful for the presentation and materials themselves to be universally designed. This serves as a model and engages the community in the benefits of the approach. Often, you do not need to create mechanisms for communication. Articulate the communication methods with which you already engage. Integrate the introduction and implementation of UDL into them. For example, if you have developed or regularly attend local access television, highlight UDL implementation in the classroom in a number of segments. Host community and parent forums, coffees, and gatherings and share information about UDL and what its benefits are. Include information in weekly or monthly newsletters and blogs about UDL. Distribute the information in manageable chunks and create materials that work for each particular audience. A strategy that defines its work within the culture and context of the community takes into account the community's specific culture of learning and the priorities they have (Mathews, 2014).

The efforts to engage the community in the idea of UDL within the mold of overall district strategy is such that they become partners in the promotion of the idea, but also in the funding of it. As budgets shrink, we look to alternative funding streams to sustain and grow our programs (Weerts & Hudson, 2009).

Multiple Means of Action and Expression

Research has shown that when you connect UDL into the greater district vision and strategy work, it engages more community members. Lane, Bishop, and Wilson-Jones (2005) discuss the strategy as driving the district's work in areas of goals, objectives, and activities, but is further-reaching in terms of how the school district functions and where resources are spent, based on data-driven priorities. One way to garner support for UDL is to get your school board or school committee engaged in this work. By tying UDL into the district's mission and goals, the board begins to become an important support for the work.

As a governing body, the school board works with "long-term, big-picture issues about values and beliefs, mission, vision, and goals—the community's core values. School boards are uniquely qualified to address these owner concerns because they are elected, volunteer citizens who can engage their neighbors in these important conversations about the community's purposes for its schools and the resources the community is willing to provide for its schools" (Illinois Association of School Boards, 2013, p.10).

This work must not only be framed in the beginning to engage the community, but throughout its implementation and scaling-up efforts. To do this, we must understand the need to heighten the salience of the goals and objectives of this work by continuing to reference the community-developed vision for which the goals are based, and define progress toward those goals as measurable rewards for our efforts.

We must keep the work in the community and send reminders of the goals and their value, as well as the importance of the sustained efforts. We must also counter public opinion when it pushes back against this vision, and not get sidetracked with distractions. We must engage families and the wider community in working groups throughout the implementation process. This active participation makes the work important to them. The success of UDL becomes their success, and the house we build becomes their home.

Afterword

*I*n the introduction, we shared the work of Sharma (2014), an industrial engineer, who designed a platform to allow companies to build multilayer forests in concrete jungles. His prototype guides others to create new ecosystems in barren lands. Because he has implemented this platform successfully, we now know what is possible. We hope that by sharing the resources in this text, we too have shown you what the UDL framework is capable of accomplishing when implemented throughout a five-stage process. This text focuses on the first three stages, which are meant to build a solid foundation and the frame of a house that will stand up to the test of time.

Throughout this text, we have shared a lot of resources with you. The task of leading a movement toward Universal Design for Learning (UDL) using the principles of UDL may feel daunting, since it is a multiyear commitment that will not erect a house overnight.

In the introduction of this book, we highlighted the phases of UDL implementation. During the beginning phases, you are working to investigate UDL as a potential system-wide decision-making framework, building awareness about UDL with key players within and outside of the system, and determining willingness and interest of staff to begin district UDL implementation.

By reading this book, you have built an initial understanding of UDL. You have learned how to use an evidence-based decision-making model in your school or district. You have been provided guidance in drafting a needs assessment and logic model. You have seen ways in which UDL can be incorporated into strategic thinking and integrated into an overall district strategy. You have been provided models for creating comprehensive UDL professional development. You have been asked to consider the implications of applying UDL in the classroom. You have explored how to run universally designed meetings and given consideration to offering community engagement around UDL. By simply reading this book, you have already begun to construct your UDL home. Congratulations!

For continued support during the first three stages of UDL implementation, we will be publishing additional activities and resources in a companion guidebook, *Resources for Implementing Universally Designed Leadership*. When you're ready to optimize and scale UDL as a district-wide framework, a second volume, *Universally Designed Leadership: Next Steps*, will focus on the Scale and Optimize phases, which will support you as you beautify the house you have built. Look for these titles coming from CAST Professional Publishing, along with the revised and expanded version of *UDL Now!*, Katie's practical guide for teachers on how to apply UDL in the classroom.

Appendix

UDL Rubrics

The Bartholomew Consolidated School Corporation (BCSC) has incorporated UDL practices as the single biggest percentage of their educator evaluation framework (50 percent). BCSC does this explicitly by incorporating UDL into all of the educator rubrics (including for administrators). Figures 7.1–7.3, reproduced in this appendix at full size, show the rubrics that are used in BCSC's process. These evaluation rubrics represent expectations for UDL for teachers, as well as leaders.

BCSC 2014-15 TEACHER SUCCESS RUBRIC

TEACHER BEING EVALUATED

EVALUATOR

	INEFFECTIVE (1)	NEEDS IMPROVEMENT (2)	EFFECTIVE (3)	HIGHLY EFFECTIVE (4)
UDL / INSTRUCTIONAL FRAMEWORK	€ The goal is not posted	€ The goal is posted but not addressed or instructional methods are not aligned with the goal	€ The goal is posted and instructional methods and materials align with the goal	€ The goal is posted, attainable and accessible. Instructional methods and materials align with the goal
	€ Potential barriers are not considered during the planning of the lesson or the design of the learning environment	€ Potential barriers are considered but the teacher is not applying that knowledge to the lesson plan	€ Potential barriers are considered and the teacher applies that knowledge to the learning environment	€ Potential barriers in the curriculum and learning environment are identified and addressed in the design of the lesson and the learning environment
	€ Content and skills are presented without options and scaffolding	€ Content is presented with few options and skills are presented without scaffolding	€ Content and skills are presented in multiple ways with options but with minimal scaffolding	€ Content and skills are presented in multiple ways with options and scaffolding available
	€ Students are not engaged	€ Students are engaged in relevant learning opportunities	€ Students are engaged in relevant and meaningful learning opportunities	€ Students are engaged in authentic, relevant, and meaningful learning opportunities
	€ Students do not interact with or demonstrate content and skill comprehension	€ Students interact with content and skill comprehension but do not demonstrate knowledge	€ Students interact with and demonstrate content and skill comprehension in multiple ways	€ Students consistently interact with and demonstrate content and skill comprehension in multiple ways

Figure 7.1: Sample BCSC evaluation rubrics

BCSC
2014-15 DEAN/COUNSELOR SUCCESS RUBRIC

DEAN/COUNSELOR BEING EVALUATED _____

EVALUATOR _____

INSTRUCTIONAL FRAMEWORK — UDL	INEFFECTIVE (1)	NEEDS IMPROVEMENT (2)	EFFECTIVE (3)	HIGHLY EFFECTIVE (4)
	€ School wide goals are not known	€ School wide goals are known but not addressed or instructional resources are not aligned with the goals	€ School wide goals are known and instructional resources align with the goal	€ School wide goals are known, attainable and accessible. Instructional resources align with the goal
	€ Potential barriers are not considered during the planning of the interaction or the design of the learning environment	€ Potential barriers are considered but the building administrator is not applying that knowledge to the interaction	€ Potential barriers are considered and the building administrator applies that knowledge to the learning environment	€ Potential barriers related to the resources, information, and learning environment are identified and addressed in the design of the interaction and the learning environment
	€ Content and skills are presented without options and scaffolding	€ Content is presented with few options and skills are presented without scaffolding	€ Content and skills are presented in multiple ways with options but with minimal scaffolding	€ Content and skills are presented in multiple ways with options and scaffolding available
	€ The students and/or parents are not engaged	€ The students and/or parents are engaged in relevant learning opportunities	€ The students and/or parents are engaged in relevant and meaningful learning opportunities	€ The students and/or parents are engaged in authentic, relevant, and meaningful learning opportunities
	€ The students do not demonstrate and articulate appropriate choices	€ The students rarely demonstrate and articulate appropriate choices	€ The students occasionally demonstrate and articulate appropriate choices	€ The students consistently demonstrate and articulate appropriate choices

Figure 7.2: Sample BCSC evaluation rubrics (continued)

BCSC
2014-15 BUILDING ADMINISTRATOR SUCCESS RUBRIC

ADMINISTRATOR BEING EVALUATED _____

EVALUATOR _____

		INEFFECTIVE (1)	NEEDS IMPROVEMENT (2)	EFFECTIVE (3)	HIGHLY EFFECTIVE (4)
INSTRUCTIONAL FRAMEWORK	UDL	€ School wide goals are not known	€ School wide goals are known but not addressed or instructional resources are not aligned with the goals	€ School wide goals are known and instructional resources align with the goal	€ School wide goal are known, attainable, and accessible. Instructional resources align with the goal
		€ Potential barriers are not considered during the planning of the interaction or the design of the learning environment	€ Potential barriers are considered but the building administrator is not applying that knowledge to the interaction	€ Potential barriers are considered and the building administrator applies that knowledge to the learning environment	€ Potential barriers related to the resources, information and learning environment are identified and addressed in the design of the interaction and the learning environment
		€ Content and skills are presented without options and scaffolding	€ Content is presented with few options and skills are presented without scaffolding	€ Content and skills are presented in multiple ways with options but with minimal scaffolding	€ Content and skills are presented in multiple ways with options and scaffolding available
		€ The school community members are not engaged	€ The school community members are engaged in relevant learning opportunities	€ The school community members are engaged in relevant and meaningful learning opportunities	€ The school community members are engaged in authentic, relevant and meaningful learning opportunities
		€ The school community members do not interact with or demonstrate content and skill comprehension	€ The school community members interact with content and skill comprehension but do not demonstrate knowledge	€ The school community members interact with and demonstrate content and skill comprehension in multiple ways	€ The school community members consistently interact with and demonstrate content and skill comprehension in multiple ways

Figure 7.3: Sample BCSC evaluation rubrics (continued)

References

Alexander, M. (2015). From the ground up: Foundations. *This Old House.* Retrieved from *www.thisoldhouse.com*

Averill, O. H., & Rinaldi, C. (2011). Multi-tier system of supports. *District Administration, 47*(8), 91.

Brooks, M. (2015). What's up with gravity? *New Statesman.* Retrieved from *http://www.newstatesman.com/2015/05/what-s-gravity*

CAST (2011). *Universal design for learning guidelines* version 2.0. Wakefield, MA: Author.

Charmaz, K. (2003). "Grounded theory." In: Smith, J. A. (ed.), *Qualitative psychology: A practical guide to research methods*, pp. 81–110. London: Sage.

Cox, A. (2014). Increasing purposeful communication in the workplace: Two school-district models. *The Delta Kappa Gamma Bulletin, 80*(3), 34–38.

Curtis, R. E. & City, E. A. (2009). *Strategy in action: How school systems can support powerful teaching and learning.* Cambridge, MA: Harvard Education Press.

The Danielson Group (2013). *The Framework for Teaching.* Princeton, NJ: Author.

Emerson, R. W. (1870). *Society and solitude: Twelve chapters.* London: S. Low, Son & Marston. Also online at *http://www.bartleby.com/90/0701.html*

Evans, C., Williams, J. B., King, L., & Metcalf, D. (2010). Modeling, guided instruction, and application of UDL in a rural special education teacher preparation program. *Rural Special Education Quarterly, 29*(4), 41–48.

Every Child Succeeds Act of 2015. (2015). Pub. L. 114–95.

Frechtling, J. (2007). *Logic modeling methods in program evaluation.* San Francisco, CA: John Wiley & Sons.

Frye, A. W., & Hemmer, P. A. (2012). Program evaluation models and related theories: AMEE Guide No. 67. *Medical Teacher, 34*(5), e288–e299.

Geier, R., & Smith, S., (2012). *District and school data team toolkit.* Everett, WA: Washington Office of Superintendent of Public Instruction, Washington School Information Processing Cooperative, and Public Consulting Group.

Harlacher, J. E., & Sanford, A. (2015). *Distinguishing between Tier 2 and Tier 3 instruction in order to support implementation of RTI.* New York: National Center on Learning Disabilities. Retrieved from rtinetwork.org

Hill, S. (2012). *Leap of faith: A literature review on the effects of professional development on program quality and youth outcomes.* Wellesley, MA: National Institute on Out-of-School Time.

Illinois Association of School Boards (2013). *Connecting with the community: The purpose and process of community engagement as part of effective school board governance.* Author.

Johnson, E. (2015). *How to develop an effective Tier II System.* The National Center for Learning Disabilities. Retrieved from rtinetwork.org

Kantha, L. (2012). What if the gravitational constant G is not a true constant? *Physics Essays, 25*(2), 282–289.

Kekahio, W., Cicchinelli, L., Lawton, B., & Brandon, P. R. (2014). Logic models: A tool for effective program planning, collaboration, and monitoring. (REL 2014–025). Washington, DC: U.S. Department of Education, Institute of Education Sciences, National Center for Education Evaluation and Regional Assistance, Regional Educational Laboratory Pacific. Retrieved from *http://ies.ed.gov/ncee/edlabs*

Lacity, M. C., & Willcocks, L. P. (2014). Nine practices for best-in-class BPO performance. *MIS Quarterly Executive, 13*(3), 131–146.

Lane, R. J., Bishop, H. L., & Wilson-Jones, L. (2005). Creating an effective strategic plan for the school district. *Journal of Instructional Psychology, 32*(3), 197–204.

Lawton, B., Brandon, P.R., Cicchinelli, L., & Kekahio, W. (2014). Logic models: A tool for designing and monitoring program evaluations. (REL 2014–007). Washington, DC: U.S. Department of Education, Institute of Education Sciences, National Center for Education Evaluation and Regional Assistance, Regional Educational Laboratory Pacific. Retrieved from *http://ies.ed.gov/ncee/edlabs*

Lopez, M. E, & Caspe, M. (2014). Family engagement in anywhere, anytime learning. *Family Involvement Network of Educators (FINE) Newsletter, 6*(3). Retrieved from *http://www.hfrp.org/publications-resources/browse-our-publications/family-engagement-in-anywhere-anytime-learning*

Love, N., Stiles, K. E., Mundry, S. E., & DiRanna, K. (2008). *The data coach's guide to improving learning for all students: Unleashing the power of collaborative inquiry.* Thousand Oaks, CA: Corwin Press.

Massachusetts Department of Elementary and Secondary Education. (MA DESE). (2012). *Massachusetts model system for educator evaluation: Appendix B. School-level administrator rubric.* Malden, MA: Author.

Massachusetts Department of Elementary and Secondary Education. (MA DESE). (2015a). *Educator effectiveness guidebook for inclusive practice:* Malden, MA: Author.

Massachusetts Department of Elementary and Secondary Education. (MA DESE). (2015b). *Educator evaluation data: Student growth percentiles, race/ethnicity, gender, and professional teaching status.* Malden, MA: Author.

Massachusetts Department of Elementary and Secondary Education. (2015c). *District data team toolkit: Helping districts establish, grow, and maintain a culture of inquiry and data use.* Retrieved from *http://www.doe.mass.edu/apa/ucd/ddtt/toolkit.pdf*

Massachusetts Department of Education (2015). The Massachusetts Model System for Educator Evaluation (Part III: Guide to Rubrics and Model Rubrics for Superintendent, Administrator, and Teacher; Appendix C. Teacher Rubric). Updated from original 2012 version. Malden, MA: Author. Retrieved from *http://www.doe.mass.edu/edeval/model/PartIII_AppxC.pdf*

Mathews, D. (2014), Rethinking civic engagement: The case of the public schools and the public. *National Civic Review, 103,* 4–10.

Meyer, A., Rose, D. H., & Gordon, D. (2014). *Universal design for learning: Theory and practice.* Wakefield, MA: CAST Professional Publishing.

Moore, D.S. & McCabe, G.P. (1998). *Introduction to the practice of statistics, 3rd edition.* New York: W. H. Freeman and Company.

National Center for Education Statistics. (2011). *SLDS best practices brief. Stakeholder communication: Tips from the states.* Washington, DC: US Department of Education.

National Center on Universal Design for Learning. (2012). UDL implementation: A process of change [Online seminar presentation]. UDL Series, No. 3. Retrieved from *http://udlseries.udlcenter.org/presentations/udl_ implementation.html#*

National Governors Association Center for Best Practices & Council of Chief State School Officers. (2010). *Common Core State Standards.* Washington, DC: Authors.

NGSS Lead States. (2013). *Next Generation Science Standards: For states, by states.* Washington, DC: The National Academies Press.

National School Reform Faculty. (2015). Retrieved from *http://www.nsrfhar-mony.org/*

Pawson, R., Boaz, A., Grayson, L., Long, A. & Barnes, C. (2003). Types and quality of knowledge in social care. Knowledge Review 3. London: SCIE.

Reeves, D. B. (2008). *Assessing educational leaders: Evaluating performance for improved individual and organizational results* (2nd ed.). Thousand Oaks, CA: Corwin Press.

Rose, D.H., & Meyer, A. (2002). *Teaching every student in the digital age: Universal design for learning.* Alexandria, VA: ASCD.

Roy, S., & Singh, S. (2015). Strategic planning for management of technology: An empirical study with Indian steel sectors. *Vision, 19*(2), 112–131.

Shakman, K., & Rodriguez, S. M. (2015). *Logic models for program design, implementation, and evaluation: Workshop toolkit.* National Center for Education Evaluation and Regional Assistance.

Shakman, K., & Rodriguez, S. M. (2015). *Logic models for program design, implementation, and evaluation: Workshop toolkit* (REL 2015–057). Washington, DC: U.S. Department of Education, Institute of Education Sciences, National Center for Education Evaluation and Regional Assistance, Regional Educational Laboratory Northeast & Islands. Retrieved from *http://files.eric.ed.gov/fulltext/ED556231.pdf*

Sharma, S. (2014). *How to grow a tiny forest anywhere.* [video file]. Retrieved from *https://www.ted.com/speakers/shubhendu_sharma*

Sivers, D. (2010). How to start a movement. [video file]. Retrieved from *https://www.ted.com/talks/derek_sivers_how_to_start_a_ movement?language=en*

Stone, D., & Heen, S. (2014) *Thanks for the feedback.* New York: Viking.

Torma, C. (2015). The planning commission's contribution to the capital improvement plan. *Planning, 81*(2), 49.

U.S. Department of Education, Office of Educational Technology. (2016). Future ready learning: Reimagining the role of technology in education, Washington, DC: Author.

Van Horn, G. (2015, November). Bartholomew's elevated path leads through UDL. *School Administrator 72*(10), 33.

Weerts, D., & Hudson, E. (2009). Engagement and institutional advancement. *New Directions for Higher Education, 147,* 65–74.

Wei, R.C., Darling-Hammond, L., & Adamson, F. (2010). *Professional development in the United States: Trends and challenges.* Dallas, TX: National Staff Development Council.

Weisbord, M. & Janoff, S. (2016). Future Search Network [Website]. Retrieved from *http://www.futuresearch.net/*

Index

Acknowledgments

Writing a book about leadership wouldn't have been possible without my leadership mentor, my work BFF, and my coauthor, Dr. Kristan Rodriguez. Kristan encouraged me to transition from the classroom to a leadership position and has supported me ever since. She embodies all the characteristics of a universally designed leader. She tirelessly works for what is best for all students, collaborates with all stakeholders to create thoughtful strategy to move our district forward, and is a model of the power of commitment when it comes to overcoming obstacles. Her patience, class, and persistence are nothing short of exceptional.

I'd also like to acknowledge David Gordon, director of publishing at CAST, for always supporting the next item on my bucket list and providing mastery-oriented feedback to improve my writing. I also appreciate that he makes sure I have access to the most current research in the field of UDL to ensure my practice evolves as we learn more about the best way to meet the needs of all learners.

Finally, to my husband Lon: for every goal I aspire to, he is an integral part of my strategy. Because of his unwavering motivation, the endless entertainment he provides for our four kids so I can write, the text messages that make me laugh so hard my stomach hurts, and chai tea latte deliveries, he is the best decision I ever made.

—Katie Novak

I would be remiss not to begin by acknowledging Dr. Katie Novak for being a guide and a partner in this pursuit. I very much looked forward to our weekend writing adventures. I never quite knew when one of our contributions ended and the other's began. It was a natural and synchronous process. I am also thankful for the professional partnership we have in our daily work. Your genius in the workplace is a constant inspiration.

To Claire Sheff-Kohn, my coach and friend: you modeled what a strong successful woman superintendent can be.

To my colleagues in Groton-Dunstable: I have much to share at our administrative retreat this year. Spoiler alert: the theme is superheroes.

To Rafael Rodriguez, my husband, whose love and sacrifice helped me get where I am today, both professionally and personally. You have been my everything since I was 18, my husband since I was 19, and my parenting partner since I was 20.

To my children, Rafael, Xavier, and Gabriel:, you are the inspiration for this book. The importance and impact of effective administrative practices on the education of our children is not to be taken lightly. Every time I see the spark in your eyes, I know my work has meaning.

To Diane Scinto, for being the model of what a mother should be. Your care and encouragement have always been what I needed, when I needed it.

To Daniel Scinto, who has not only served as my loving father, but as my professional mentor. Thank you for being the foundation on which I have built my practice.

—Kristan Rodriguez

About the Authors

Katie Novak is the assistant superintendent of the Groton-Dunstable Regional School District in Massachusetts, and one of the country's leading experts in Universal Design for Learning (UDL). With many years of experience in teaching and administration, Novak designs and presents workshops both nationally and internationally focusing on implementation of UDL and the state standards. She holds a doctorate in curriculum and teaching from Boston University.

She is the author of the best-selling book on inclusive education, *UDL Now! A Teacher's Guide to Applying Universal Design for Learning in Today's Classrooms,* and the coauthor of *UDL in the Cloud! How to Design and Deliver Online Education Using Universal Design for Learning,* both published by CAST Professional Publishing.

Kristan Rodriguez is superintendent of the Groton-Dunstable Regional School District. She earned a Ph.D. in educational administration from Boston College, and has had a successful career as an administrator since 2001. Her career spans preschool through university, where she has worked in public and private settings alike. Dr. Rodriguez has presented nationally on leadership and learning for the past 15 years. In both her speaking and writing, she draws upon her experience as a central office administrator, building administrator, teacher, and professor.

CPSIA information can be obtained
at www.ICGtesting.com
Printed in the USA
LVHW021134031120
670572LV00004B/242

9 781930 583627